Trade Secrets

Meredith® Books
Des Moines, Iowa

Trade Secrets:

Insider Advice on Creating Your Own Personal Style

Editor: Vicki L. Ingham

Project Manager/Writer: Jean Schissel Norman

Contributing Editors: Susan Andrews, Carla Howard, Laura Hull, Sally Mauer, Sandra Mohlmann, Joetta Moulden, Barbara Mundall, Amy O'Keefe, Hilary Rose

Senior Associate Design Director: Mick Schnepf

Graphic Designers: Chad Johnston, Joe Wysong, Conyers Design, Inc.

Copy Chief: Terri Fredrickson

Copy and Production Editor: Victoria Forlini

Editorial Operations Manager: Karen Schirm

Managers, Book Production: Pam Kvitne, Marjorie J. Schenkelberg, Rick von Holdt, Mark Weaver

Contributing Copy Editor: Stacey Schildroth

Contributing Proofreaders: Becky Etchen, Sue Fetters, David Krause, Brenda Scott Royce

Contributing Photographers: Gordon Beall, Fran Brennan, Cheryl Dalton, Michael Garland, Bob Geenspan, Jamie Hadley, Jon Jensen, Jenifer Jordan, Janet Mesic Mackie, Robert Mauer, Dan Piassick, Beth Singer, Thomas Veneklasen

Indexer: Beverley Nightenhelser

Editorial and Design Assistants: Kaye Chabot, Karen McFadden, Mary Lee Gavin

Meredith® Books
Editor in Chief: Linda Raglan Cunningham
Design Director: Matt Strelecki
Executive Editor, Home Decorating and Design: Denise L. Caringer

Publisher: James D. Blume
Executive Director, Marketing: Jeffrey Myers
Executive Director, New Business Development: Todd M. Davis
Executive Director, Sales: Ken Zagor
Director, Operations: George A. Susral
Director, Production: Douglas M. Johnston
Business Director: Jim Leonard

Vice President and General Manager: Douglas J. Guendel

Better Homes and Gardens® Magazine
Editor in Chief: Karol DeWulf Nickell
Deputy Editor, Home Design: Oma Blaise Ford

Meredith Publishing Group
President, Publishing Group: Stephen M. Lacy
Vice President-Publishing Director: Bob Mate

Meredith Corporation
Chairman and Chief Executive Officer: William T. Kerr

In Memoriam: E. T. Meredith III (1933-2003)

All of us at Meredith® Books are dedicated to providing you with information and ideas to enhance your home. We welcome your comments and suggestions. Write to us at: Meredith Books, Home Decorating and Design Editorial Department, 1716 Locust St., Des Moines, IA 50309-3023. If you would like to purchase any of our home decorating and design, cooking, crafts, gardening, or home improvement books, check wherever quality books are sold. Or visit us at: bhgbooks.com

Cover Photograph: Jon Jensen

I didn't start out to redecorate the three-season porch at my house. After 20 years of writing about home, I've learned to focus on editorial deadlines and postpone my own decorating projects. But not this time.

Photographs for *Trade Secrets* began gathering on my desk and the inspiring words of the 24 featured design entrepreneurs—product designers, interior designers, shopkeepers, and photo stylists—filled my files. I could barely keep from jumping up from my computer and tearing into my porch project. It's not surprising. Although these designers create style for others, it's in their own homes that they reveal their clearest design vision and most personal style. It's a fun glimpse into their creative world and an inspiring exposure to design ideas that will change the way you think about your own home.

It certainly changed *my* view at home. Halfway through the book I gave in. I'd return from errands with a handful of paint chips and fabric swatches, perfect for a porch redo. I found my porch plans changing in concert with their advice. After several designers suggested editing what you put in a room, I grabbed storage boxes and turned a writing break into the first step of my project. I bought just enough expensive fabric for two pillows and used inexpensive cotton duck for the chair cushions. The search for one-of-a-kind objects sent me to the antiques mall nearby. New paint colors appeared as oversize checks on the porch floor.

Jumping into a project is exactly the reaction I hope you experience with this book, whether you read one story from start to finish or focus on a nugget of advice in the "Get the Look" feature. You'll find tips you can use in a spare 15 minutes or advice that will guide you through a top-to-bottom room remake. You'll learn how to fill a bookcase, arrange flowers, design a slipcover, or plan a floor pattern. You'll discover how to combine textures, patterns, and colors. And you'll see that designers have different styles and budgets, just like you and your friends.

Ready to see how their advice stacks up in real life? Turn the page to be inspired.

Jean Schissel Norman

3

contents

product designers

Product designers imagine what can be, then spend months and sometimes years making it happen. The insatiable urge to create drives them to constantly modify their work. Their collective experiences fuel the fire with fresh concepts and worldly inspirations. New ideas set them on the less-traveled path. It all unites in that moment when they're sitting at a worktable drawing what might be. Home for these creative doers is part design laboratory and part design retreat. One thing is sure: Home is never a finished project.

"I rarely find inspiration when I go looking for it. It's usually when I'm out that it finds me."

—GREGORY EVANS, GREGORY EVANS, INC., TEXTILES

"I don't have a favorite color. Any color used in the right situation would be beautiful."

—BRAD HUNTZINGER, IRONIES AND OLY, FURNITURE AND ACCESSORIES

"A true creative person is never satisfied with what they do."

—GREGORY EVANS, GREGORY EVANS, INC., TEXTILES

Brad Huntzinger
furniture and accessories designer

Ironies and Oly

BERKELEY, CALIFORNIA

nature at his doorstep

Brad Huntzinger favors an eclectic mix of finishes and styles. In the living room new pieces (the sofa, coffee table, and console) are from his furniture line, Oly. Natural objects, such as shells, rocks, and horns, add a touch of the outdoors. **Opposite:** New ceramic pieces in three soft colors look like sculpture on top of a cabinet. Brad likes to create subtle displays that don't scream for attention.

wisteria seedpods, shells of every size and shape, and a rock with a hole in it—they're the pieces of nature designer Brad Huntzinger brings home to his California cottage. But they're not just objects he stuffs in his pocket on a quiet walk and forgets once he's home.

"Those things remind me that no matter what I design, it is not as good as what is out there already in nature," he says. For a reminder, he hangs these offerings from nature on hooks above his front door where he sees them every day.

Brad repeats the patterns, textures, and shapes of nature in the furniture and accessories he designs with his business partner, Kate McIntyre. Their two home furnishings lines, Ironies and Oly, offer pieces such as sconces and frames covered with shells, ceramics in the shapes of vegetables, and consoles with doors of sliced bamboo.

To produce the affordable Oly line, Brad spends a third of the year in Indonesia or Vietnam. While there he works on prototypes and quality control and searches out new materials to use in the line. "We're always seeing new things to inspire us," Brad says.

The constant search for new ideas has its drawbacks when it comes to finishing a home, however. "Favorites change," Brad says. "That's one of the problems with designers in their own homes. We know we're going to fall in love with something new next week." Trends, too, can divert a designer. "I'm susceptible to them, but I try to resist them," he says. He notes the popularity of orange and, lately, of acid yellow. He may try them at home, he says, but he's not ready to bring them into his design work.

For now Brad lives with a palette of subtle and cool colors, and a mix of styles that suits his wandering soul. Bringing work home means sitting down on a French-inspired sofa upholstered in raffia and putting his feet up on a modern zinc-wrapped coffee table. Brad likes to mix pieces from his product lines with found objects and his own artwork. "I believe in eclecticism and interiors that surprise you and are interesting," he says.

His search for beauty usually leads him off the beaten path. The discovery might be an old statue from Java or rocks from the beach. "They're not something someone else tells you is beautiful," he says. "You're turning away from mass culture." That's exactly where Brad finds the look that's right for him.

Brad says small rooms look best with
a carefully edited selection of furniture
and objects. He keeps most surfaces
spare, then gathers a collection—here,
of glass bottles—for impact.
Opposite: A bedside stand offers
the perfect display space for favorites.
A second table holds the lamp.

BRAD HUNTZINGER

An eclectic mix of updated classics and natural objects in a tiny cottage

▶ Start with an eclectic mix. For Brad that means combining styles, such as a modern metal coffee table with a French settee or an sparkly mirror with a rustic wood table, *above right*. "Have fun trying out different combinations," he says.

▶ Use subtle colors. Brad chooses cool hues, such as blues and greens, for his home. "If I use brown, it's a green brown instead of a red brown," he says. He also prefers muddy colors that are muted and subdued.

▶ Play with scale. "Rooms need big things and little things, tall things and low things," he says. He might set a big globe on a small table or hang a chandelier in a little room. "It makes people think of things a little differently." Don't be afraid to push the limits on scale: Brad places a four-poster bed that stretches almost to the ceiling in a tiny room, *opposite*. "It makes the room feel larger," he says. For a muted backdrop Brad turned the books so their cream-colored pages face out.

▶ Let the light in. "Light is absolutely critical to a space," he says. "It gives it life." He leaves most windows bare but uses simple panels made of translucent cotton voile over some windows. "I'd rather have light and not have the privacy," he says.

▶ Paint the floors. Wood floors painted black anchor the rooms. For light-starved rooms, paint floors off-white.

▶ Bring the world home. Brad constantly collects items from the beach, the mountains, flea markets, and travel, *above center*. "Some of my favorite things most people wouldn't look at twice," he says. That includes a bottle of moldy oak balls and a collection of crab shells that he loves for their colors and textures.

▶ Keep interiors understated. "I like it when things reveal themselves over time versus wanting your attention the minute you go into a house," he says. The easiest way to achieve this look is with subdued colors. The final effect should be calm.

▶ Add textural contrast. Think in terms of texture as rough and smooth or even as old and new, says Brad. The contrast might be rough rocks on a painted table or velvet against a worn wood arm. "I find this kind of contrast surprising, fun, and beautiful," he says.

NATURAL OBJECTS

SEASHELLS

▶**SEASHELLS.** "They're magic," he says. "They housed animals, but they're beautiful, streamlined, and curved. They're the stuff we can't make." Brad places a single shell on a table or clusters groups in baskets.

▶**ART.** Most of the paintings are his own work and include small landscapes and large abstracts. He displays them informally, hanging a finished canvas without any framing or propping a landscape painted on cardboard against a wall.

▶**BOOKS.** In the guest room Brad places books on the bookshelves so the pages, not the spines, face out (see page 15). "I'm giving up something for the visual [effect]," he admits. He did try the books with the spines out but didn't like the way they looked. Now they create a wall of texture behind the bed. He claims he can easily find the book he wants. "You remember a book by its size."

▶**PILLOWS.** Pillows add a spot of color to Brad's rooms. In the living room the striped pillows are made from velvet ribbons. Kidney

pillows sit on the chairs. "Pillows are about comfort and that's what a house should be about," he says.

▶**A LINEN-COVERED CABINET.** Brad built this cabinet 20 years ago for a showhouse. Now it's home to a display of Oly ceramics. "It's a piece I've always had in my house that I still like," he says.

▶**CERAMICS.** New ceramic pieces in muted tones of celadon, lime, and white show how Brad combines similar objects for

GLASS

impact. "You get to have fun with shape and color," he says.

▶GLASS. Brad loves glass because you can see through it and yet it reflects. "It becomes almost like water," he says. Massing glass pieces on a surface creates drama, whether on the dining table or atop dressers and side tables.

▶NATURAL OBJECTS. Brad likes the subtle contrast of natural objects against manufactured pieces. It allows him to make small changes at no cost on a regular basis.

BUSINESS BASICS
Brad and his business partner, Kate McIntyre, created the Ironies line 15 years ago. This high-end line offers custom furniture through designer showrooms.

They started the Oly line, *above*, a few years ago to reach customers who wanted a clean, livable, stylish look that's also more affordable. To keep the prices down, they build the furniture overseas and limit the choices of finishes and materials to three or fewer. "Oly is really based on taking classics and simplifying them," he says.

OLY
  PHONE 510/644-1870
  WEBSITE www.olystudio.com

IRONIES
  PHONE 510/644-2100

Ann Sacks

tile entrepreneur

retired president and creative officer of Ann Sacks

PORTLAND, OREGON

modern by design

Above: *Ann Sacks bought the mid-20th-century modern furniture at two house sales. Bamboo trees in concrete planters screen the windows.*

Opposite: *New Knoll chairs in yellow complement the vintage magenta chairs and warm up the modern space.*

19

some designers might be tempted to spread their favorite family photographs around the house, arranging a dozen on a living room table and a few more on the mantel. For Ann Sacks, however, these sentimental images become a dramatic piece of art when they're gathered in one space and framed identically with crisp white mats and narrow black frames.

There's no denying it. Ann gets the big picture.

It's the same with the line of tile and cut stone that bears her name. An individual Ann Sacks tile is beautiful. But it's in a room of installed tile that Ann's big-picture view becomes apparent. "I really try to look at tile as architecture," she says.

That's why she loves to see a small space, such as a powder room, completely encased in tile, or every inch of a kitchen backsplash paved with tile. She specifies grout lines so narrow they all but disappear. Plan the installation, she cautions, as carefully as the product decision. After all, beautiful tile can be harmed by too many cuts. "I really believe that less is more," she says.

Her design philosophy also extends to the modern apartment she shares with husband, Robert. She picked one stone, Princess Yellow limestone, for the floors throughout the main living area. French Blue limestone covers the kitchen countertops and living room fireplace. Glass mosaic tiles in a random mix of neutrals blanket

Above left: White fabrics and paint give the master bedroom a serene, undecorated feeling.
Below left: "The kitchen is efficient," says Ann. "It looks like a place where food is prepared." The cabinets mimic furniture from the 1950s.
Opposite: Limestone floors and walls paved in oversize subway tiles showcase Ann's look. The tulip chairs and table were designed by Eero Saarinen.

most of the walls in the master bathroom. Of course Ann followed her own design advice. She used large quantities of a few materials, kept the grout lines thin, and even had the flooring laid before building the walls to minimize cuts in the 4×2½-foot stone slabs.

A modern apartment dressed in stone and tile in a new steel-and-glass building could seem cold. It isn't, however, because the house is about family and is filled with things Ann collects and loves.

"My house is very simple," she says. "It has family photos as art and things that I have bought for thirty years at street sales and other unsophisticated and inexpensive venues."

That includes her amazing collection of midcentury modern furniture. She purchased the pieces at two house sales and admits she decided to buy them after just a brief glimpse. "The items were affordable and simple, but also had a unique point of view from a period that had been largely unsuccessful commercially," she says.

She still uses the pieces today, some in their "as found" condition. That includes magenta upholstery on the original Knoll chairs, a Charles and Ray Eames sofa for Herman Miller, Eero Saarinen tulip chairs and table, and bentwood side chairs by William Stephens for Knoll. She added other pieces as well, including paintings and glass pieces by modern artists, always mindful that her contemporary apartment demands simplicity.

"I love the fact that the decor is very simple," Ann says, "that everything is here because it gets used. Nothing is here just to look at. Except for the paintings on the walls."

ANN SACKS

A restrained palette of stone and tile plus 1950s furniture in a modern apartment

▶ Keep backgrounds minimal. Ann chose tile, stone, and paint in a range from oatmeal to gray, *above center*. "In my house the backgrounds recede," she says. She simplified the look by using just a few materials in the apartment.

▶ Warm with color. When she bought the vintage Knoll chairs, they were covered in magenta upholstery. She added new Knoll chairs in bright yellow. Both colors work in a modern space, Ann says. "Magenta

and yellow are probably two of the warmest colors in the palette."

▶ Keep an open feeling with just a few walls. Ann's home is so open you can see the entire apartment from the front door. It requires discipline to keep out clutter.

▶ Fill the space with modern furniture. Ann admits it took her about 10 minutes to make the decision to buy a collection of midcentury modern furniture from a house sale. "The items were affordable and simple," she says.

▶ Take advantage of light. That meant leaving 13-foot-tall windows uncovered to scoop in every last ray of sunshine. At night off-white drapes draw shut.

▶ Use accessories sparingly. That means minimal accent pieces, no rugs, and just a few art pieces. This spareness suits Ann.

ANN'S TILE TIPS

▶ Use a lot of tile. "It is more important to use a lot of tile and stone than to install 'special' or costly materials," Ann says. That's why she covers kitchen and bath backsplashes from the countertop to the cabinets, and sometimes to the ceiling, *opposite*. "In a small room like a powder bath, it is a wonderful feeling to clad all the walls all the way up," Ann says.

▶ Minimize grout lines. To do this Ann suggests the "absolute minimum grout joint" and a grout color close to the color of the tile or stone, *above right*.

▶ Use authentic tile or stone. If you want the look of a French cottage, buy reclaimed materials of that vintage through tile showrooms. "Authentic materials are far more effective in conveying a feeling than are products executed to mimic the real thing."

ART OBJECTS

PENDANT LIGHTS

▶**FAMILY PHOTOS.** Plain metal channels stacked four high provide the perfect gallery for Ann's photographs of family and friends. Ann framed the photos with crisp white mats and pencil-thin black frames. By massing the photos, she turned an assortment of black and white photographs into one piece of art.

▶**ART OBJECTS.** Ann uses a few well-chosen vases made by Patrick Crespin on the shelves adjacent to the fireplace. The yellow glass bowl was a gift from a friend in France and made by his friend in Limoges. Ann says you can collect things on trips even if you live in a minimalist house. "You have to be disciplined about how you use

them," she says. Bringing a new piece into the mix usually involves some creative rearranging of what you have.

▶**ORIGINAL PAINTINGS.** Ann has favorites that she uses throughout her home, most bought locally in Portland. The oversize piece above the fireplace resembles stone but is an abstract painting.

▶**BAMBOO.** A row of potted bamboo trees screens the living room windows from a busy corner. "They have a great impact on the naturalness of the apartment," Ann says. The trees are potted in concrete planters. White drapes pull shut behind the bamboo at night.

▶**EVERYDAY DISHES.** Open shelves in the kitchen let Ann keep everyday dishes out where they're just a reach away.

▶**1950S TABLES.** Tubular metal legs and glass tops make small tables almost disappear in the rooms. Ann often places a single object as a focal point on a table.

▶**PENDANT LIGHTS.** Hanging lights by Patrick Crespin offer three-dimensional art above the dining table and in the stairwell.

▶**A PIECE THAT MAKES HER SMILE.** Ann bought Big Boy, the hamburger icon, in Chicago. She spied it in a vendor's office and made an offer.

EVERYDAY DISHES

1950S TABLES

BUSINESS BASICS
Ann Sacks retired in 2003 from the position of Creative Officer at Ann Sacks. She's in the incubation phase of a new business, one that she just can't talk about yet. Ann started her first business much the same way, with a simple idea that took the marketplace by surprise.

She didn't start out to reinvent the way tile was made and sold. A former teacher and social worker, she simply fell in love with some tiles at a local shop. It wasn't long before she was selling tiles out of her home, soon followed by the introduction of a new line of tile available at retail showrooms.

Her concept was new: Create custom tile and treat it like an architectural product. That meant matching tile colors to bathroom fixtures and carpeting. Kohler purchased Ann Sacks in 1989.

To learn more about the tile programs Ann created, check out the product line at the company she founded. Showrooms, like the one in Portland, Oregon, *above,* provide ideas and products.

ANN SACKS
PHONE 503/281-7751
WEBSITE www.annsacks.com
(For a list of showroom locations and phone numbers.)

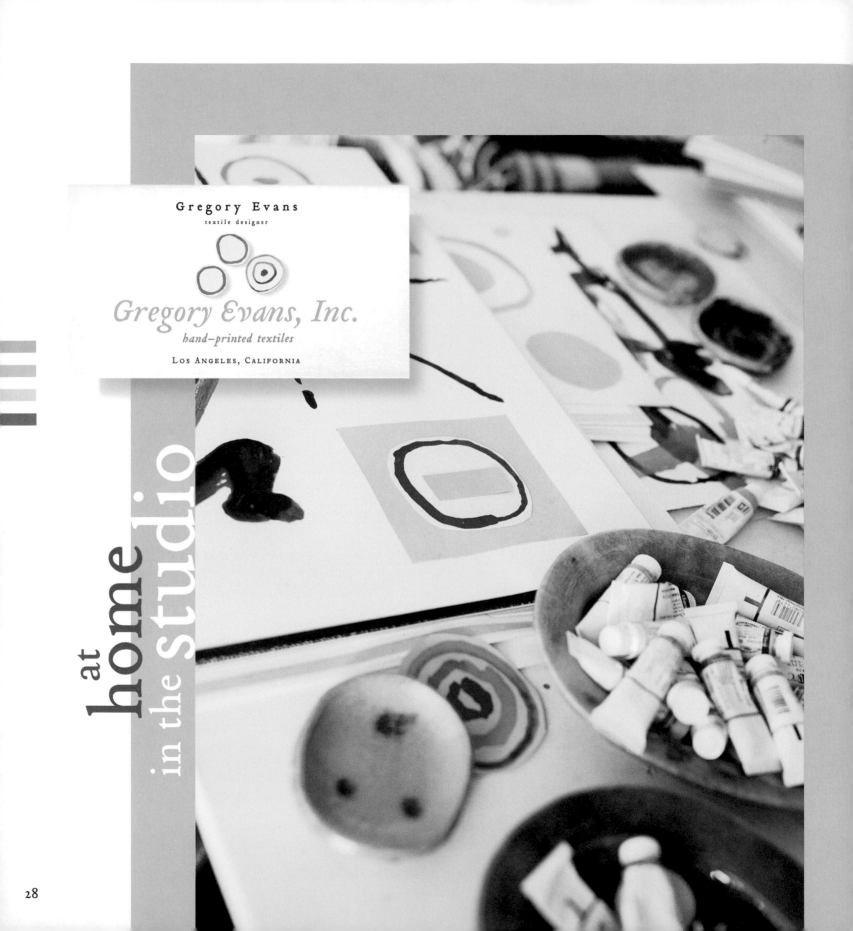

Gregory Evans
textile designer

Gregory Evans, Inc.
hand–printed textiles

LOS ANGELES, CALIFORNIA

at home in the studio

Gregory Evans designs textiles in the
same space where he lives so he brought
in three identical tables for working and
soft chairs for the moments between.
Favorite inspirational objects surround
him on every surface.
Opposite: Flexible work surfaces hold
paints where they're handy whenever
an idea strikes.

Bookshelves throughout the house store books and other objects Gregory collects. He made the shades from his own fabric. Upholstered chairs provide seating flexibility.

Opposite above: A worktable, one of three in the living room, holds a current project. Gregory surrounds himself with inspiration by stacking artwork on the tabletops and tacking it to walls.

Opposite below: Gregory collects objects for their shapes and colors. He's quick to remove pieces that no longer inspire his art or please his designer's eye.

living

living in a design studio makes perfect sense to textile designer Gregory Evans. After all, the small 1920s bungalow where he works is also his home. "It's not a separate life for me," he says. "I work where I live."

Gregory doesn't spend every minute working. It's just that his work surrounds him at home wherever he turns. "Instead of living in a decorated home, my home is an active studio and workroom," he says.

Three worktables in his living room hold the tools of his trade—paints, papers, and brushes. Wood and upholstered chairs offer plenty of sitting space. The bookcases throughout store inspiration, everything from art books to pieces of pottery, but in a visually organized way. "Things aren't just stuck in a random place," he says. "It has to be harmonious."

The textile designs Gregory paints find their way, temporarily, to the walls. Living with the colorful patterns is a crucial part of his creative process. "Things I thought were really good, I become dissatisfied with," he says. "Others I didn't like as well I may find more interesting."

That's the case with a design he propped against a bookshelf two months earlier. He didn't think it really worked when he first created it, but now he plans to make it into fabric. "It's only having it across the room from me every morning that made me want to turn it into fabric," he says.

Gregory first introduced his hand-printed fabrics in 1990. His designs feature strong colors, ethnic shapes, and irregular stripes, dots, and triangles. Someone once told him that his textiles look sort of Scandinavian-African. "Oddly enough they are," he says. "I have been inspired by both over the years."

Drawing inspiration from the world he's exposed to and bringing it home to his little compound in California suits Gregory just fine. "Being a creative person I have tried many different ideas and looks that I've wanted to go with and the kind of house I've wanted to live in." Although he loves the look he has achieved in his home/studio, he knows change is inevitable. "I'm always introducing new things into what I'm doing," he says. "A true creative person is never satisfied."

GREGORY EVANS

Part home, part studio, totally inspiring

▶ Start with warm neutral tones. For Gregory that means warm white paint on the living room walls and a warm violet on the ceiling. In the bedroom he used a dark neutral brown, a color he finds soothing and grounding. "I love color, and I used to paint my walls strong colors, but sometimes that's very limiting to what you can do later on," he says.

▶ Add pops of strong color. Gregory uses his own textiles as well as other accessories and fabrics to add color. He pins up his own painted designs so he can live with them for a while. He also uses fabrics made from his designs and pins them to a wall or window frame, *opposite,* or makes them into Roman shades.

▶ Fill your rooms with art. Favorite posters and paintings by artists such as David Hockney and Alexander Calder slip between samples of his own work. "I put art pieces where they look good, where I feel comfortable looking at them," he says. Some hang, others lean against walls.

▶ Build shelves. "I'm not a collector of things I don't use or don't like," he says. Everything he gathers fuels his design work. He keeps all the objects carefully arranged on shelves, *above center.* The combinations offer as much inspiration to Gregory as the objects.

▶ Provide spaces for sitting and working. In a living/working space there has to be room for both. Gregory had three white tables custom-built for the living room. Then he added upholstered chairs that cluster around the tables or gather to seat guests. "I don't have any furniture in the house that I don't use," he says. He loves working at tables, moving between them throughout the day. "If I had a bigger house, I would just have more tables," he says.

▶ Add your own touch to everything. He may paint bold stripes on a lampshade, *above right,* pin a painted pattern to the edge of a bookcase, or drape vintage blankets over a chair. A lampshade that "sticks out too much" for Gregory's liking right now will fit in once he has a chance to tone it down with paper collages and watercolors.

BOLD TEXTILES

OUTDOOR TABLE AND CHAIRS

►**BOOKS.** Gregory sets books horizontally as well as vertically in white bookcases. Some provide pedestals for other favorite finds such as vintage pottery or artwork.

►**CALIFORNIA POTTERY.** Although Gregory isn't a collector, he has found himself drawn once again, after 20 years, to the shapes and colors of this 1920s to 1930s pottery. Collecting by color and shape helps build a cohesive look.

►**POSTERS AND PAINTINGS.** He has posters by favorite artists such as Miró, Calder, and Matisse. He also has a copy of

his portrait done by artist David Hockney. Gregory worked with Hockney on set design. "But mostly I have my own work," he says. He stacks and layers framed pieces on surfaces where they're easy to move.

►**BOLD TEXTILES.** From the Beacon blanket on his bed to the Indian rugs in his living room, Gregory uses bold textiles for their simple designs and strong colors.

►**INSPIRATIONAL OBJECTS.** They might be found objects or pieces he picks up at a shop that sells vintage items. When he buys something, it's purely aesthetic. "I'm not

looking for valuable things. I'm usually not even interested in the history," he says. "I'm buying inspiration." Then he uses the pieces to create vignettes on bookcases and tables.

►**BASIC WINDOW COVERINGS.** Window coverings in Gregory's house have to be simple and adaptable. After all, he constantly changes them. He either makes Roman shades and leaves them down or pins pieces of his own fabric or designs painted on paper to the window frames. "It's temporary," he says. "I like to see different fabrics at different times." This suits his working style perfectly. Using

POSTERS AND PAINTINGS

BOOKS

ART PROJECTS

simple, no-sew treatments is a great way to add flexibility to any room's look.

▶**OUTDOOR TABLE AND CHAIRS.** The balmy climate of southern California lets Gregory use his outdoor spaces like indoor rooms. A table and a chair are all he needs to get comfortable and creative.

▶**ART PROJECTS.** Naturally Gregory's art projects occupy his working home/studio. Everything from bolts of his own fabric stacked in a corner to a lampshade he painted with irregular stripes gives him the ability to personalize his space.

BUSINESS BASICS
The fabrics Gregory Evans designs feature simple graphic patterns that look part African, part Scandinavian. "The fabrics are a total of everything I look at or have looked at, everything that I enjoy," he says.

The look is really about geometrics created with not-so-perfect lines and shapes. "There is something very fundamental about a line, a dot, a square, or a circle," he says.

Gregory combines these elements to create designs for fabrics and rugs. The fabrics are printed on natural fibers, including cotton, linen, and hemp. His current projects include a line of indoor/outdoor fabrics printed on solution-dyed acrylic.

GREGORY EVANS, INC.
PHONE 323/656-7300
WEBSITE www.gregoryevans.com
(for showroom locations
and phone numbers)

"When people see liberal use of bright color, they get brave."
—VIRGINIA BURNEY, VIRGINIA BURNEY DESIGNS

interior designers

An interior designer has to like working with people as much as he or she loves design. The job requires the people skills of a psychologist, the tutoring talents of a teacher, the business sense of a marketer, the questioning tactics of a journalist, and the ability to combine shape, color, texture, and pattern into spaces that clients call home. Interior designers spend long days at work creating rooms for others, but they express their own sense of style most purely at home.

"Clean lines, fewer things, better things."
—ELIZABETH GIBSON-WAKEMAN,
ELIZABETH GIBSON-WAKEMAN INTERIORS

"*I love doing the unexpected, putting fine things with not necessarily fine things, rough with smooth, texture with gloss.*"

—HENRY BROWN, HENRY BROWN INTERIORS

"*I don't want things to have a time and a place. I want things to look like they evolved.*"

—FORD BOYD BAILEY, FORD BOYD INTERIORS

mastering the mix

Stephen Bedford
shopkeeper

West Coast Plant Co.
accessories and planted containers for home

PORTLAND, OREGON

Henry Brown
interior designer

Henry Brown Interiors

PORTLAND, OREGON

Henry Brown and Stephen Bedford like
to mix styles and finishes throughout
their house. In the music room, Chinese
figures blend with architectural pieces.
Opposite: Instead of using the family
room for its intended purpose, Henry
and Stephen turned it into a dining
room that easily seats 16 at two tables.
For small gatherings, they use just one
table. Lampshades mounted upside
down provide lighting. "The shades
create intimacy because they're so low,"
Henry says. For parties they replace the
orchids with low floral arrangements.

china

dinnerware doesn't exist in matching sets in the Portland, Oregon, home of interior designer Henry Brown and shopkeeper Stephen Bedford. But don't think that Henry and Stephen haven't gotten around to shopping. In fact, says Henry, it's all part of the plan. "For me," Henry says, "it's fun to mix it up a bit. The real love and passion I have is about combining things."

On the tabletop that means pairing lacquer rice bowls with green chopsticks and setting them on black-banded china plates. For a client's home the combination might include Queen Anne chairs around a parsons dining table. At home Henry really perfects the mix, blending modern with traditional, Chinese with French, big scale pieces with small accents.

It all works against a monochromatic color scheme of putty, cream, raffia, pale gray, sand, celadon, khaki, and white. "When I see rooms in those quiet colors, I'm always drawn to them," Henry says.

Creating the backdrop is the first step. "You have to have the spaces right before you go about furnishing them." Oh sure, says Henry, you can disguise some dated architectural elements. But that's not the path he took with his 1960s architect-designed home. Henry and Stephen bought the house in 1999, then spent a year remodeling it. They used an architect and a kitchen designer, both instrumental in interpreting Henry's vision. "I understand what makes a house good and bad. They know how to get it there."

With its 9-foot, 4-inch ceilings and 8-foot, 4-inch doors, the home had the grand scale of an old house but with modern touches such as grain-matched walnut cabinetry in the kitchen, 3-foot squares of white terrazzo on the floors, hard-finished plaster, and doorways with chamfered edges. The pair replaced the home's dated aluminum sliders with wooden French doors, removed walls so they could see through the house, restored terrazzo floors they

Left: *The sofa anchors one of the living room's seating areas. Henry covered the sofa in linen and, for a little sheen, added bolsters in slipper satin. Artwork picks up the colors used throughout the space. An old zinc finial, one of a pair, stands guard at one side of the home's entry.*
Opposite: *Henry custom-designed this tall-back sofa to separate the living room from the front entry. "You feel sheltered when you sit in it," he says.*

Because the living room is a large space, Henry divided it into several seating areas. Small tables placed around the room provide easy spots to set a drink. The custom-built cabinets flanking the fireplace store media gear, including the television. Black serves as an accent color, appearing as pillow fabric, lamps, and Ming vases on the cabinet tops. Henry hung the draperies from the ceiling to stretch the vertical look of the room; see-through blinds soften the light.

found under vinyl and carpet, and reconfigured the living areas.

Then Henry set about furnishing the new spaces. Oversize upholstered pieces, most covered in solid-color linen, grace every room. The pieces reflect the mix Henry loves—some French, some modern, some vintage. The upholstered furniture presents an asymmetrical arrangement. Henry introduces symmetry with matching tables and cabinets, incorporating pairs of accessories such as Ming jars, candlestands, and lamps.

And he adds a bit of fun. The shades over the dining tables are hung upside down and finished with oversize tassels. "I love doing the unexpected," Henry says. And he loves perfecting the mix.

Above: A pillow covered in tiger-striped velvet adds a note of luxury to the linen-covered antique chaise. A ceramic garden stool serves as a small table.

Opposite: For a serene bedroom Henry upholstered the entire wall, not just the headboard, with linen that matches the wall paint. Crisp white bedding adds contrast. Monkey prints, hung en masse, create one large piece of art. Clear glass lamp bases disappear in pools of light.

STEPHEN BEDFORD
AND HENRY BROWN

A sophisticated mix
of modern and
traditional styles set
against a neutral
color palette

▶ Select a monochromatic color scheme. Henry and Stephen's color palette includes putty, cream, raffia, gray, sand, celadon, khaki, and white. Slight variations in tones create serene spaces.

▶ Weave an accent color throughout. In their house, that can be as simple as charcoal. For a client Henry might use Chinese red for fabric and accessories. "If you use the color in different ways, it reads [as] less predictable," he says.

▶ Mix it up. Putting fine things with not necessarily fine things, rough with smooth, and texture with gloss adds energy. Henry uses contemporary art with period furniture or vintage pieces in a modern bookcase, *above center*.

▶ Opt for scale. "I love grand gestures when it comes to scale," Henry says—big altar candleholders, large architectural elements, and oversize paintings. "Large things give a room a less predictable look," he says. But vary the scale too. If everything is large it can look crazy.

▶ Create vertical lines. "Most spaces we live in today need vertical elements." He suggests taking draperies to the ceilings and using floor-to-ceiling mirrors. Even the cooktop hood stretches up, *opposite*.

▶ Use solid fabrics for upholstery. Fabrics with pile—mohair, chenille, and corduroy—are soft to the touch and look great in solids. Linens and ducks are practical but not as soft.

▶ Custom cushions. It's important to give cushions the right "sit," Henry says. That means all-feathers for a firmer cushion, a 50-50 mix of feather and down for a throw pillow, and 75 percent feathers for a back pillow.

▶ Create symmetry for balance. Pairing furniture and accessories works easily, *above right*. "To be able to mix it up as much as I like to, there has to be symmetry," he says. "Know the rules so you can break them."

▶ Be playful. Henry points to the arm wall sconce hung between the dining room windows (see page 38). "I love things with a sense of humor," he says.

▶ Put sisal underfoot. Its rough texture contrasts with smooth terrazzo floors.

ASIAN ANTIQUES

LITTLE TABLES

►**LUXURY PILLOWS.** If you can't afford fabulous fabrics on everything, splurge on a small amount of silk or cut velvet for wonderful pillows.

►**LITTLE TABLES.** Henry places them in front of an armless sofa, by a bed, or alongside a chaise or chair to hold a drink and a book. They're easy to move wherever you need them. The tables vary in style from vintage ceramics to modern metals.

►**ASIAN ANTIQUES.** "I've collected them since I started collecting," he says. His Chinese and Korean ceramics include pillows in the form of cats, vessels of different shapes and sizes, Han dynasty figures, and a coromandel screen.

►**CANDLES AND CANDLESTANDS.** Many are altar candlestands. Henry likes to use large groupings of candles in the living room and dining room. "They add a wonderful light quality," he says.

►**FLOOR LAMPS.** It's not always possible to use large-scale chests or tables next to chairs to place a lamp. Floor lamps give you light and free up table space.

►**COLLECTED PRINTS.** Botanical, monkey, and architectural prints are favorite collections. The monkey prints hang closely spaced so they look like one big piece of art.

►**ARTWORK.** "I'd still keep the pieces and rotate them even if I moved into a smaller space," he says. He frames the art simply so the painting is the focus.

►**INTERIOR PLANTS.** Henry loves to use large trees for their scale and blooming orchids for their beauty. They're also part of the mix that Stephen sells at his shop, West Coast Plant Co.

►**OVERSIZE ACCESSORIES.** For Henry it's all about scale. He uses architectural elements over a bar, opts for Ming jars to top a pair of cabinets, and groups altar candlestands on his coffee table.

►**RAM'S HEADS.** Look for repeats of this classic shape. You'll find a pair on the kitchen wall and another on a bedroom lamp.

LUXURY PILLOWS

BUSINESS BASICS West Coast Plant
Co. started out creating inventive planted containers for commercial interiors. They soon branched into residential work and added a store full of containers and other home accessories, *above*. The store features inspiring displays of distinctive indoor and outdoor items in a variety of styles and colors.

In his interior design business, Henry Brown Interiors, Henry loves to mix modern and traditional pieces. It's the look he is known for throughout the Portland area. Although his look at home is done in neutrals, he also works with restrained use of color in clients' homes.

WEST COAST PLANT CO.
ADDRESS 1825 NW Vaughn
Portland, Oregon 97209
PHONE 503/227-6500
WEBSITE www.westcoastplant.com

HENRY BROWN INTERIORS
ADDRESS 108 NW 9th Ave., Suite 202
Portland, Oregon 97209
PHONE 503/274-0966

Below: *Carrie Raphael likes to mass simple objects in single file. She also collects mirrors, especially big old ones.* **Opposite:** *To keep the living room from feeling too sweet, Carrie used a strong pastel on the walls, crisp white on the trim, and an edited collection of new and vintage furniture.*

the fashionable farmhouse

pink and aqua walls, chandeliers, and slipcovered chairs might look sweetly soft and purely romantic in Carrie Raphael's Maryland home. But a closer look reveals a decorating style that's meant to work as hard and look as beautiful as the Victorian farmhouse she calls home. This young designer knows that style and utility can form a perfectly delightful design marriage.

"I never feel the need to hide a room's purpose," Carrie says. "I love open shelves in kitchens and baths. I find beauty in piles of simple white washcloths and stacks of dishes neatly piled high."

This utilitarian beauty also shows up in slipcovers that slide into the wash when too many smudges leave a less-than-fresh look. In the kitchen and entry, she painted bare floors to a soft sheen with patterns that hide the tracks of daily life.

Carrie credits many design influences, none more than Swedish artist Carl Larsson, who died decades before she was born. She discovered his paintings of home life when she was 18, spending hours poring over the watercolors of his family doing chores, getting ready for lunch, or just hemming a dress. Sometimes he captured just the finished rooms. (See some of these paintings at the official Larsson website: www.clg.se.)

"They loved their home and took great care in personalizing their space," says Carrie. The Scandinavian design sensibility of spare interiors filled with light and colorful rooms that offer easy comfort stayed with her.

Now she pairs the simple beauty of Scandinavian style with her own love of fashion. Carrie admits that when she's looking through fashion magazines, she's imagining how a detail from a dress—a line of buttons, a pleat, or a bow—can be used on a slipcover.

"I love clothing," Carrie says. "I like the details you find on dresses, and I like to use those details on pillows and slipcovers."

Right: Carrie cut down an old table for the library so children's chairs would fit under it. The chandelier, once electrified, now holds candles. Slipcovered chairs and a love seat offer easy care. Carrie loves to sit here and browse through her design books.
Opposite: Old slipcovered chairs snuggle up to the new dining room table. Carrie picks pieces based on shape, then alters them with paint or fabric. She removed the old stove but left the fireplace mantel. Salvage pieces top the doorways.

Open shelves add hardworking style to this unfitted farmhouse kitchen. The island is an old bakery worktable Carrie scrubbed, bleached, and sanded.

Even her favorite blue pillow was once a sweater. She knew it would make the perfect pillow, soft and pretty, when she bought it. It's not surprising that she never wore the sweater, but loves the pillow she made from the fabric.

Carrie describes design elements in fashion terms, comparing lampshades to little dress forms and a favorite chair slipcover to a 1920s woman's skirt. She treats chairs like one-of-a-kind dressmakers' mannequins, dressing them to call attention to a shapely leg or a well-formed back. That's why you'll find kicky box pleats on the bottom of one slipcover and covered buttons on the back of another.

Vintage fabrics play a big part in how she dresses new and old furniture frames. The vintage fabrics are placed for impact. "You want to see the fabric when you walk in the room," Carrie says.

If the fabric is fragile, she'll use it on the back of a piece or as a skirt where it receives the least amount of wear. Although she always adds details to slipcovers, she designs them with restraint. If you put too many details on one slipcover, none of them will stand out, Carrie says. It's the same philosophy she uses throughout her home, whether it's in carefully arranging a collection on a table or organizing furniture in a room.

Left: Carrie and her husband, Charlie, removed a wall between the kitchen and eating area to create one big family space. Painted furniture and floors, simple Roman shades, and storage baskets give her the Scandinavian look she loves best.

Below: An unfitted kitchen with minimal cabinetry works perfectly for Carrie. "I like having things around me that I can pull out," she says. She used stainless-steel base cabinets to blend with the appliances. White seemed too jarring.

Daughter Emma's room is all about color. The preschooler picked the fabric she liked, then Carrie painted the room to match. A Victorian dresser and bed look fresh with a new coat of paint. **Opposite:** Shelves and baskets make space for lots of kid gear. Carrie slipcovered two pint-size chairs with contrasting flounces. An old table, cut down to play height, provides a perfect base for Emma's dollhouse.

CARRIE RAPHAEL

Strong pastels,
soft slipcovers, and
open storage
in a Victorian
farmhouse

▶ Mix white with just one color. "I love color but not a lot of mixing of color," Carrie says. She uses a different pastel tone in every room downstairs. "Not baby pastels," she says. Because rooms, like the living room, *opposite,* are filled with light, she uses intense pastel shades and always paints the trim bright white.

▶ Slipcover one great chair frame for every room. "In every room you need an awesome chair dressed in vintage fabrics,"

she says. Slipcovers instantly relax the look of a chair, *above right.* Carrie covers the chairs with tight-fitting slipcovers of her own design. They feature dressmaker details such as box pleats, covered buttons, and flirty ties.

▶ Pair vintage and inexpensive fabrics. She picks up vintage linens to use with inexpensive cotton canvas and treats both fabrics the same way. She tosses yardage into hot water for two washings, throws it in a hot dryer with 24 sheets of fabric softener, then washes it again to remove the softener film. Finally she dries the fabric without softener sheets. The fabric will get softer each time you wash it. "Just like old jeans," she says.

▶ Paint the floors. To get the Scandinavian look she likes best, Carrie paints floors in light tones and patterns, *above center.* She preserves the paint with polyurethane.

▶ Keep window coverings basic. "I don't want anything distracting from the light that's coming in," she says. For privacy she uses simple white linen shades that pull up during the day.

▶ Combine vintage and new furniture in both wood and upholstered pieces. She alters almost everything she buys. That may mean new paint for an old cabinet or a slipcover of vintage fabric for a new sofa. The important thing, says Carrie, is to buy furniture for shape, then alter its surface or color to suit your home.

▶ Plan storage that's easy to use. "Everything should have a place and a purpose in a room," she says. She fills baskets with children's toys, places folded towels on a chair in the bathroom, nestles a reading corner next to bookcases filled with design books, and places a bench near the front door where it's handy.

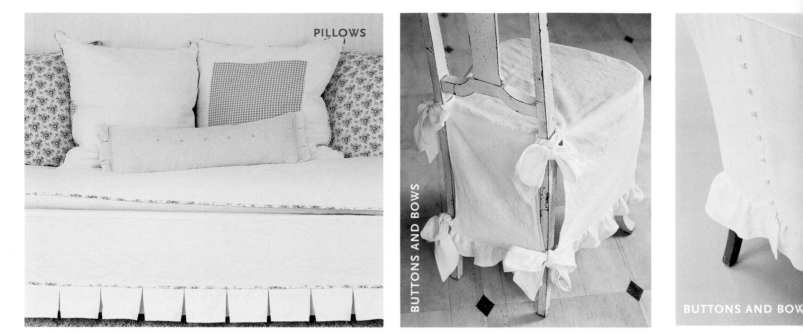

PILLOWS

BUTTONS AND BOWS

BUTTONS AND BOWS

BUTTONS AND BOW

▶ **BUTTONS AND BOWS.** Carrie can't design a slipcover without adding her signature dressmaker details. But what she does to a chair is a reflection of its style. A chair with soft curves might be treated to bows and ruffles while a simple chair could be finished with cording and a box pleat.

▶ **MIRRORS.** They're great for reflecting light. "I like old ones and large ones," Carrie says. She uses them to bring more light into her rooms and to visually open up spaces.

▶ **MULTIPLES OF FAVORITE PIECES.** Just one bucket or basket won't do for Carrie, who likes to combine these pieces. A row of farm buckets sits on a bench in her living room. At Christmas they hold small evergreen trees. "I love the same thing used over and over again," she says. "Things placed in a

row are clean, simple, and nondistracting." For a dinner party she puts flowers in low containers that stretch the length of the harvest table.

▶ **CHANDELIERS.** Don't expect a chandelier only over the dining room table. Carrie likes to hang dressy chandeliers in bathrooms, bedrooms, and even the kitchen. "My kitchen isn't fancy, but it's fun to have a chandelier there," she says. She uses candle chandeliers, especially in winter, to cast a warm glow in her living room and library.

▶ **IRONSTONE.** Carrie uses ironstone throughout her house, but keeps most of her collection on shelves in the kitchen. She loves the old pieces for their bright white color and simple shapes. She buys chipped

pieces because they give her a big look for very little money.

▶ **PILLOWS.** She places a single pillow in a chair or a row of pillows on a daybed. With kids in the house, pillows are also great for throwing on the floor for TV viewing.

▶ **PILES OF BLANKETS.** A stack of blankets that match the room wait in a handy spot so they can be pulled out when the temperature drops. It's Carrie's perfect mix of style and usefulness.

▶ **BASKETS.** She uses them throughout her house to keep clutter under control. "Baskets are a way of organizing something without putting it in a file, cabinet, or desk," she says. They're handy, too, for teaching children to pick up after they finish playing.

BUTTONS AND BOWS

MIRRORS

CHANDELIERS

BUSINESS BASICS Carrie Raphael
started designing interiors when she was just 8 years old. Of course the houses were dollsize and made from shoeboxes. But they were completely detailed down to the window treatments.

Now she works with clients to create interiors and slipcovers that reflect the style she has in her own home. Most of her clients have young families and want casual but pretty homes. "I take a practical approach. I try to understand how they're going to live in their house," she says. That means using white slipcovers for families with children because the covers easily can be bleached.

Carrie also makes a line of fabric shopping bags that combine new and vintage fabrics.

CARRIE RAPHAEL DESIGNS
ADDRESS Port Republic, Maryland
PHONE 410/586-8242 or 703/981-9854
E-MAIL raphaeldesigns@comcast.net

61

climate controlled

Elizabeth Gibson-Wakeman
interior designer

Elizabeth Gibson-Wakeman Interiors

SARASOTA, FLORIDA

Left: Elizabeth Gibson-Wakeman divided and enclosed a long screened porch to make a library for her husband and a wicker sitting room. "It's my room of my own," she says. Carved ceiling plaques salvaged from a French château hang above the 1890s wicker sofa.

Opposite: The existing pool was a plus when Elizabeth decided to buy the house. She added a formal fountain, then placed the cocktail area in the house within view of this spot.

raised

raised in New England, Elizabeth Gibson-Wakeman found her design niche 20 years ago in semitropical Florida. She didn't cast aside her traditional roots. It's just that in Sarasota she could express all the design lessons learned along the way.

"Moving to Sarasota really liberated me as a designer," Elizabeth says. "Florida is building new homes with fresh ideas and with owners who come from all over the world with their particular influences."

Elizabeth usually works with clients on new homes. This allows her to influence every aspect, from the function and orientation of rooms to the location of electrical outlets. She considers the livability of the house for the owners, the climate, and the seasons.

Although her own home was built in 1922, Elizabeth applied the same design principles to its remodel. The stucco house was in sad shape, but had strong, clean lines, high ceilings, thick walls, wood floors, and large windows perfect for cross ventilation.

Working on her home was easier than working on a new house because the structure and its site were set. "I spent a lot of time judging light and shadows," she says. "It's important to create seating areas where you're going to be comfortable at the time of day you want to use them." Now an east-facing breakfast spot basks in morning light, and a cocktail area soaks up pool views.

The designer also factored in flexibility to accommodate how she and her husband live. She created two seating areas in the living room, one for four, the other for six. A large dining room is now an intimate eating spot for six, while the enlarged kitchen welcomes eight for convivial, relaxed dinners.

This studied approach to her home shows up in the details, too, with six to nine shades of white paint in every interior. Elizabeth loves elegant fabrics and uses the most colorful pieces for pillows. And she surrounds herself with all her favorites—faux bamboo furniture from the late 19th century, elegant 19th-century French pieces, original paintings, and orchids.

Above: Elizabeth added on to create a 22×22-foot kitchen with room for guests. A large island separates the working side of the kitchen from the eating area. A warming oven and drawers for linens face the table.

Opposite: Elegant drapes dress up the kitchen. "I spend a lot of time in my kitchen and I want it to feel as good to me as all the other rooms," she says. She painted the custom cabinets a soft gray rather than white, which she says is too hard to maintain.

Club and slipper chairs cluster around an upholstered ottoman. "I put my feet up on it," she says. The French chest is one of a pair that she bought from a Sarasota estate. "If you have one or two good antique pieces in a room, they'll make the room," she says.

ELIZABETH GIBSON-
WAKEMAN

Architectural details and elegant French pieces in a classic Florida house

▶ Let form follow function. It's crucial to consider how you actually live in rooms, not how you think you should use them. Make sure there's a comfortable chair by the fireplace for reading, a breakfast room facing east to catch the morning sun, and furniture that comfortably seats the size crew you usually invite for dinner.

▶ Start with a neutral background. Elizabeth used nine shades of white paint in her house. In her dining room, *opposite,* she painted

the three-piece crown molding with three shades of white, the walls and ceilings only slightly darker than the molding paints, and the doors in another shade of white. To get the color just right, Elizabeth tests a quart of paint at a time, spreading it on vertical and horizontal surfaces. "The light in a house changes the look of the color," she says.

▶ Add a touch of your favorite color. Elizabeth loves muddy greens and uses them for a punch of color. She saves the strongest colors to use in the smallest amounts, usually on tables, small chairs, and pillows, *above right.*

▶ Layer texture. Light dances on wood and silk. If you have a lot of wood, use some silk, then throw in a heavy woven fabric. "It's a balance between what sheds light and what absorbs light," she says. "Good rooms need both."

▶ Keep wood floors dark. The refinished floors throughout feature a 1920s favorite, a color she calls dark tobacco. She likes the way it silhouettes furniture.

▶ Opt for less. Elizabeth's mantra: Clean lines, fewer things, better things. "In order to enhance something, you have to surround it with open space," she says.

▶ Collect vintage wood furniture, *above center.* "If you have one or two good antique pieces in a room," she says, "they'll make the room." Buy good pieces and trade up as your budget allows.

▶ Start with new upholstered pieces. The old frames, she explains, were built for small people and are often uncomfortable. "Buy good new upholstered pieces because you can make them look however you want them to look based on the fabric," she says.

FAUX-BAMBOO FURNITURE

ORIGINAL ART

▶ELEGANT FABRICS. "The difference," says Elizabeth, "is always apparent." She loves silks and linens. For upholstery she selects a fabric blend of silk and cotton—silk for the sheen and cotton for strength. She uses colorful fabrics in small amounts.

▶SOFT LIGHTING. "So many things that are wonderful can be destroyed by harsh light," she says. She uses nothing brighter than a 60-watt bulb in all the lamps, except for reading. She puts black halogen reading lamps next to reading chairs and 4-inch can lights in the kitchen. Add lighting where you need it and always put it on a dimmer so you can adjust the light, she says.

▶FLOWERS AND MORE FLOWERS. "Buy as much as your budget allows and put them in every room in your house," Elizabeth says. She loves orchids because a plant lasts five or more months. Favorite cut flowers include tulips (because they follow the sun) and old-fashioned delphiniums.

▶SIMPLE WINDOW TREATMENTS. Some windows are bare. Others Elizabeth covers with vertical curtain panels and shades for privacy. "Don't choke your windows, allow them to breathe," she says.

▶ITALIAN LINENS. Elizabeth buys new linens in shades of white. "They're so pristine and crisp," she says. To give them impact, she masses a collection of linen towels in a bathroom.

▶ORIGINAL ART. As a collector of vintage and new artwork, Elizabeth cautions against buying decorator paintings. "There are so many good artists producing art today," she says. Use your money to buy an original. Then frame it simply. You shouldn't look at a painting and notice only the frame. If Elizabeth buys a framed vintage painting, she generally leaves the frame intact.

▶FAUX BAMBOO FURNITURE. Elizabeth's love of faux bamboo and vintage

FRENCH POTTERY

ITALIAN LINENS

ELEGANT FABRICS

furniture strikes an appropriate note in Florida's semitropical climate. She uses most of her collection in the master bedroom.

▶SISAL RUGS. Textured sisal rugs provide a counterpoint to Elizabeth's fine antiques. "Sisal is strong and soft at the same time," she says. "It can stand up to a wonderful old piece." Most of her wood floors are bare.

▶FRENCH POTTERY. A huge French pottery bowl holds a collection of fruits grown on trees in Elizabeth's yard. "Fruit becomes my fresh bouquet of flowers in the kitchen," she says.

BUSINESS BASICS For Elizabeth interior design starts before one line is drawn on a blueprint. She works alongside the homeowners, architect, and construction people to get every detail right. "By the time I get to the furniture, I've been working with the same people for a year and a half," she says. She believes in educating her clients and giving them appropriate choices. "You have to be a good resource person," she says.

ELIZABETH GIBSON-WAKEMAN INTERIORS

ADDRESS 1600 Hyde Park
Sarasota, Florida 34239

PHONE 941/955-1636 or 207/644-6518

71

Mark Clay
creative director

Ralph Lauren
Home Collection
NEW YORK, NEW YORK

industrial style

72

Elements of industrial style—poured concrete floors, metal-grid stairs, and an enclosed ceiling fan from a stadium-supply firm—point to the factory past of Mark Clay's Dallas loft. To soften the space he added sea-grass rugs over the concrete, hung linen curtains above the original window frames, and brought in warm woods and leather.

Opposite: A wall of shelves opposite the living room sofa holds Mark's favorites: books, black-and-white drawings and photographs, and storage boxes.

Left: Metal drawers from an auto-supply company hold linens and flatware in Mark's dining room. He topped the wood table with galvanized metal. The chairs are old but have a fresh coat of black paint.

Opposite: Mark likes to mix handsome vintage pieces with modern tables and accessories. It gives him the contrast between dull and shiny, and smooth and rough that he prefers. The linen drapes feature a deep hem of cotton canvas.

creative

director Mark Clay sees and designs it all. "I have to create so many different looks for Polo/Ralph Lauren," he says. A store might feature a Scottish hunt lodge and a Provence cottage for six months, then an Elizabethan manor and an American seaside house the next six months. Mark researches and plans the design and shops for vintage items to use in the sets. "I learned to do everything," he says.

Before his recent move to New York, Mark's home was a space of his own design, a look he loved and lived with for more than five years. His loft featured an open area that he divided into a living room, dining room, and kitchen, plus a mezzanine for the bedroom and bath. The building's structure—concrete floors and columns, a metal staircase, and brick walls—dictated the design.

To complement the industrial background, Mark stacked metal parts bins as a cupboard in his dining room, installed a caged ceiling fan in his living room, and used old electrical pipes for curtain rods.

Then he brought in soft textures for furnishings and floors. "This loft has a very industrial feeling and lots of hard surfaces," he says. "It made sense for me to balance that hardness with natural elements such as leather, linen, sea grass, wood, brushed metal, and a neutral palette."

Linen curtains edged with canvas, sea-grass rugs, and leather seating introduced texture and warm color. The casual, neutral environment was perfect for Mark.

"After seeing so much and acquiring so much for my work all day long, it is refreshing to come home to a clean palette void of color."

MARK CLAY

Metal and concrete paired with warm woods and leather in a city loft

▶ Start with a loft space. That's the ideal first step, says Mark, although it's not always possible. To create this look in a standard home or apartment, look for spaces with ceilings higher than 8 feet and rooms large enough to hold some big pieces of furniture.

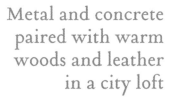

▶ Create a backdrop that works with the look. Start with hardwood floors and a neutral palette of gray, taupe, and cream for walls and furniture.

▶ Put a little black in every room. Mark uses paint, fabric, building materials, and accessories to give each room a touch of black. For a style punch, paint window frames and muntins black.

▶ Bring in metal. A floating metal staircase adds drama to Mark's loft. You can get the look of architectural metal by selecting furniture in stainless steel and galvanized metal. Smaller pieces, such as metal lamps, a caged overhead fan, and storage boxes, can start your interior on the way to an industrial look.

▶ Opt for oversize elements. Not everyone can have windows that stretch 15 feet high, but you can drape your windows from floor to ceiling to add a sense of height to the space. Bring in large pieces of furniture, such as an oversize sofa, rather than a love seat, and bookcases that stretch from floor to ceiling.

▶ Warm up modern furniture with texture. Select aged leather and nailhead detailing to give a new sofa a vintage look. Consider waxed wood finishes to disguise the age of a table.

▶ Add sheen with glass. Mark likes to use glass for shelves and tabletops.

▶ Place sea-grass carpeting over concrete floors. The texture warms the space and defines areas in an open loft.

▶ Create a focal point with a wall of shelving. Mark used a glass and metal system that stretches up the 15-foot-tall wall opposite the sofa. The wall of storage corrals clutter but keeps things handy.

▶ Edit your accessories. Mark includes bold accessories to add warmth and style to his loft. He masses collections so they don't get lost in the lofty volumes.

SIMPLE DRAPES

INDUSTRIAL PIECES

▶BLACK AND WHITE ART. Mark collects both photography and drawings, but always in black and white. He displayed his collection by placing a row of three photographs over the sofa, stacking two on the dining room wall, and layering others among books and collections on the bookshelf wall.

▶BOOKS. He studies books in his work and makes room for them throughout his home. Bookshelves stretch up the living room wall opposite the sofa. Books are stacked on almost every available tabletop.

▶MODERN LAMPS. Lamps in Mark's loft range from paper shades with an Eastern flair to high-tech metal lamps. He varies the shapes and sizes, using some on tabletops, others on the floor.

▶INDUSTRIAL PIECES. New and vintage pieces with an industrial look complement the loft's character. In Mark's dining room, old metal drawers from an auto-supply company hold linens and flatware. He kept a draftsman's stool by his kitchen counter and an office chair by his desk; both are vintage pieces. Mark brought in new items including a caged fan and pharmacy lamps.

▶GLASS VASES. Mark loves white and cream flowers, arranging them in clear glass containers in large modern shapes. His bed even has a built-in glass vase.

▶SIMPLE DRAPES. Floor-to-ceiling drapes soften the edges of the metal window frames. Grommets on the drapes' top edges slide over plumbing pipe. He added a deep hem of brown cotton canvas to visually anchor the drapes.

▶BASIC FRAMES. Artwork, framed with a narrow band of metal or wood in a natural finish or black paint, fits the clean, spare style of the space.

BUSINESS BASICS As creative director of the Ralph Lauren Home Collection, Mark Clay creates visual displays that showcase the home-furnishings line. He works with all the Polo stores to ensure that the look coordinates between stores. Mark loves the challenge of creating a setting for each new line of furnishings, a process that involves historic research as well as shopping antiques shows for the perfect vintage pieces.

WEBSITE www.rlhome.polo.com

Virginia Burney
interior designer

Virginia Burney Designs

Viburnum, Inc.

PORTLAND, OREGON

the well-traveled decorator

Ginny Burney extended the old brass bed to fit a queen-size mattress. She turned a Turkish wedding piece into a bedspread; the bed skirt is made of Guatemalan fabric. Ginny finds it easy to mix these textiles with vintage pine furniture because they all reflect age. **Opposite:** A garment sleeve from Pakistan and tin stars from Mexico fill a case that once held saints and candles. Ginny bought the silver, brass, and red amber hat in Turkey.

Left: *"I love the way silk looks, the way it shines and drapes," Ginny says. She uses it for pillows, window treatments, and tablecloths, including this underskirt. Topped with sari pieces, the table becomes a perfect spot for one of Ginny's arrangements. Pieces of Imari pottery serve as a lamp base and as a pot for cyclamens. A camel saddle holds books.*
Opposite: *Ginny always makes her fireplace mantels extra deep (this one measures 14 inches) to accommodate large objects. Another favorite trick is to put carpets, in this case a tribal saddle bag, over the coffee table. "You can put hot and wet things on the table without looking for coasters," she says. She loves to repeat elements, such as the flowers in the painting that reappear on the table.*

journeys

for Virginia Burney lead to places well traveled and places remote. For this intrepid interior designer, traveling offers both new experiences and the opportunity to buy. That's because in order to find the vintage ethnic pieces she loves to use in decorating, Ginny's travels take her to destinations as far-flung as Indonesia, Turkey, Turkistan, India, France, Mexico, China, and Japan. She buys for herself and for clients.

Her quest for beautiful objects started early. Ginny remembers buying a brass box inlaid with silver, brass, and copper. "I think I spent my entire allowance on it when I was seven years old," she says. "I'd still buy it today."

Now her shopping list has expanded to include hand-embroidered ethnic fabrics, English pine furniture, hand-tooled metals, and more. The objects she seeks now are more unusual than her early purchases, but they still speak to her sense of art and to her heart.

These collected objects all fit perfectly in her home displayed in one colorful room after the other. Intense color may be an antidote to Portland's renowned rainy weather, but it's more of an inner love for color that turns Ginny toward daffodil-yellow walls and textiles embroidered with reds, blues, and greens. Her 1940s architect-designed ranch essentially received a new interior with vaulted ceilings, new windows and glass doors, beefy moldings, new marble fireplace surrounds, new bathrooms, and a new kitchen.

Then she layered on color—one yellow for the master bedroom, another yellow for the kitchen, a deep red for the living room, and

Right: Ginny is still amazed by the weekend trip she and her husband, Richard Bach, took to Seattle. They found 15 pub chairs in different shops, took them home, and stripped and waxed them. Old pine is a perfect complement to the colors Ginny uses. To create a long-lasting floral arrangement, she mixes gerbera daisies, iris, snapdragons, curly willow, magnolia leaves, and laurel, then removes flowers as they fade.

Opposite: Even outdoors Ginny believes in creating a sitting spot with comfy furniture. The oil painting and dishes are stored inside when she's not using the area.

a leafy green for the dining room. Collected objects and comfortable furniture complete the look. Ginny always layers her finds. She might top a worn wood dresser with a hand-embroidered textile or fill an Imari jar with a gathering of garden flowers. "Mellow acquisitions give a look you can't get any other way," she says.

Her approach to home—strong architecture, comfortable furniture, exciting color, and exquisite collections—is the key to the success of Ginny's interior design business. Her clients trust her sense of style and her practical approach to decorating.

"When I first visit a client's home, I often say, 'We can make this better today. Would you like to?' " That first step leads to some inevitable weeding out, then deciding what new pieces to add.

Decorating wisdom comes along with Ginny's design advice. Although she loves color, she recommends neutrals for flooring and bathroom fixtures so they'll last a long time. She suggests using the same colors in your home that you regularly wear. And she cautions against buying the high-priced "hot" item of the decade that will look dated just a few years later. "Everybody has a limited amount of money to spend," she says. "That's why it's so important to really think through how you want to spend it."

GINNY BURNEY

Vintage textiles and objects from around the world against a backdrop of fearless color

▶ Use color. Ginny has always had a red living room, but she has added color to the rest of her house over the years, *opposite*. "When people see liberal use of color, they get brave," she says. If you're unsure where to start, just look in your own closet. The colors you wear can be the basis for your home's colors, Ginny says.

▶ Select good upholstery pieces. They can take a big chunk of decorating dollars, so cover them in go-with-anything neutral fabrics. Then change the look with colorful pillows or throws.

▶ Learn the art of making arrangements. Ginny always plans for high, low, and medium pieces, *above center*. She uses lifts and stands to raise objects, opts for big and small elements on the same table, and brings in flowers to add a sense of life.

▶ Use fewer but larger items. Ginny edits her selections and combines them by style or period. She likes oversize tables, sink-in seating, and large accessories such as the flower arrangement, *above right*.

▶ Repeat themes. If you spot one elephant in Ginny's home, look closer and you'll see the rest of the herd. Look, too, for vases of flowers to reflect a nearby painting.

▶ Add a few aged or less-than-perfect items to the mix. Objects that are obviously used but well-loved add a sense of history. They can be heirlooms or just collected.

▶ Buy in multiples. Several trumpet vases in different sizes or metal frogs related in color but in different shapes offer more drama than one of something.

▶ Use candles to warm up a home. Ginny puts candles in candlesticks of various sizes and materials on large trays. Glass votives are good for a lengthy party.

▶ Buy great old or antique pine furniture pieces. They create a collected look, are usually affordable, and any damage can easily be waxed away. "Buy old furniture, not worn-out furniture," she says.

▶ Add something unexpected. Hang an oil painting temporarily in an outside living area, use a saddlebag as a table runner, or mix parrot tulips with casablanca lilies.

FRESH FLOWERS

▶**REAL ART.** It can be your children's art, old paintings from a junk store, or even fine art you collect, but make it real art. Then frame it well. But don't stop at frameable art. Artist-made glass, metal, and pottery pieces also bring art home.

▶**CONTAINERS.** Ginny uses boxes, trays, bowls, and baskets to gather and display collections. Sometimes she sets a piece of sculpture on top of a stack of boxes to create more height in a display.

▶**ANIMAL FIGURES.** She incorporates animals into the arrangements she creates on bookshelves, mantels, and cabinets. "Animals

in any arrangement give it life," she says. Her collection includes birds, elephants, horses, tapirs, and ducks.

▶**BOOKS.** Stacked on a tabletop or in a bookshelf, vintage books and new books add interest to a home.

▶**ETHNIC OBJECTS.** Ginny likes a look that mixes objects from around the world, such as combining a couscous dish from Morocco, pillar candlesticks from Indonesia, and a pub chair from England. To start your collection, she suggests shopping at the best stores to learn about the pieces, then browsing through antiques stores and flea

markets for bargains. Save, too, for those really good pieces you'll love forever. "They don't need to be perfect, but they should have a little patina and history," she says.

▶**FRESH FLOWERS.** She mixes fresh flowers with sticks, berries, and other greens cut from the garden. Her list of flowers that last for a long time after cutting includes lilies, roses, zinnias, and tulips. Or buy potted performers that last months: orchids, begonias, cyclamen, or amaryllis.

▶**EXOTIC TEXTILES.** Ginny collects vintage women's handwork from different cultures. She uses the pieces in unexpected

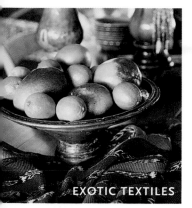

EXOTIC TEXTILES

CONTAINERS

REAL ART

ANIMAL FIGURES

REAL ART

ways, draping saris over tables, hanging embellished clothing on walls, turning mirror cloth into pillows, and placing small cloth pieces on tables. "I like fabric 'crunched' because it shows more life and pattern," she says.

▶**TRIBAL RUGS.** She spreads them on tabletops and on the floor.

▶**SILK.** "I love the way silk shines and hangs," Ginny says. She uses it for window treatments, table skirts, and pillows.

▶**STARS.** Ginny tucks stars into displays where they add a surprise.

BUSINESS BASICS After 25 years in the design business, Ginny Burney knows how to give any home a fresh look. She has a real gift for sorting through what people have, keeping the best and removing things that no longer work. She brings in color, of course, and collections. Then it's time for the fun part—deciding what to acquire. To help her clients Ginny gathers objects from around the world, then holds an annual or semiannual sale at her house. "Everything is gone in two hours," she says.

VIRGINIA BURNEY DESIGNS
ADDRESS Portland, Oregon
PHONE 503/223-1651
E-MAIL viburnum@easystreet.com

Stephen Knollenberg

interior designer

Stephen Knollenberg, Inc.

BIRMINGHAM, MICHIGAN

from town to country

At his country retreat, Steve Knollenberg
loves exaggerating the length of the
9½-foot-long dining room table by lining
up vases along the center. "It's pretty
great for a party," he says.
Opposite: In the city apartment, Steve
covered the walls in his dining room with
woven raffia. His grandmother's table,
topped with glass, fills the space. "This
is a cocktail party apartment, not a
dinner party room," he says.

Left: *Steve added bookcases and molding to the small apartment living room. If you don't have great architecture, add it, Steve says. He hung an articulating lamp above the bookcase shelves for light and drama. The English ladder is wrapped in black leather.*

Opposite: *Steve used an expensive vine fabric on the sofa pillow, then covered the sofa with affordable brushed cotton. His attention to detail shows in the Roman shades made from off-white polished linen trimmed in silk checks.*

interior designer Steve Knollenberg lives in

the best of both worlds. Weekdays he goes home to a dressy 1920s apartment in Birmingham, Michigan. Weekends he drives 2½ hours to a relaxed cottage in the woods little more than a block from Lake Michigan. Although his apartment parallels a city street and his cottage stands off the beaten path, the two homes share much.

The apartment, Steve says, is more dressy, formal, and English. The cottage interiors—more utilitarian, relaxed, and rustic—create the perfect put-up-your-feet retreat. Both places reflect Steve's list of design must-haves: good architecture, neutral backgrounds, an interesting mix of furniture, and one-of-a-kind objects.

His use of color is subtle. Steve starts with a neutral background so accent fabrics, collections, and accessories stand out. "I don't want to see a red sofa or a red wall. I want to see the bowl of red apples," he explains.

"At heart I'm sort of a traditionalist, but I like to give that style a

A room-dividing curtain of canvas bordered in suede separates the cottage's living room and dining room. "It's nice to close the room off when you're preparing for a party," Steve says. To create this sophisticated look, Steve refinished the floors to a dark tobacco color and painted the natural wall paneling white. "You could tell the house had great bones. I just simplified it." The furniture in the cottage is less expensive and more utilitarian than the furniture in his apartment. But that's not the case with the accessories, including the black lantern behind the sofa. "It's old, and it's Canadian," he says.

shot in the arm." For Steve that means giving old things a modern twist, such as upholstering a Victorian hourglass stool with black horsehair or framing a vintage flag as a giant piece of modern art.

The objects he loves the most aren't found at any mass merchandiser. Rather, he scours flea markets and antiques shops, here and abroad, looking for unique objects for both houses.

Keeping the design of his two homes separate but equal isn't as difficult as it may sound. "If I'm buying something I always think,

'Is this for the cottage or for the apartment?' " Green goes to town and black goes to the woods. The polished-linen shades trimmed in silk and French Empire chandelier? Dressy town style. Canvas drapes bordered in suede and birch branches in a clear cylinder? Perfect for a weekend getaway.

It took time and travel for Steve to find unique pieces to fill the interiors of two special places. But it's the perfect job for this weekend shopper. "I have a big passion for the find," he says.

Steve sandblasted the flagstone fireplace in the living room to remove layers of paint. He likes to use accents of black at the cottage, including this old painted chair. "It really felt like the cottage I was trying to create," he says.

Opposite: He thought about painting the den's windows but changed his mind. "When the room became white, the windows just jumped out at you," he says. Cotton duck in taupe covers the new sofa and chair. Prints of flies and dragonflies in basic frames sit on open shelves flanking the sofa.

STEPHEN KNOLLENBERG

Dressed up for a city apartment or relaxed for a weekend retreat

▶ Start with good architecture. The trick is to buy a place with good bones, then be willing to make alterations. "If it isn't in the room already, I put it in," he says. The first step is to add the right molding. Both homes feature high ceilings and interesting windows. The cottage required more vision, Steve admits. It had red paneled walls and scalloped molding.

▶ Create neutral backgrounds. That means white walls, wood floors, simple window treatments, and white slipcovers on sofas.

"Nothing is as clarifying or dramatic as shots of clean, crisp white," Steve says.

▶ Add a touch of color. Steve uses moss or leaf green in his apartment, *above center,* and black in his cottage. "I like to pick a color and then run with it," he says. He uses it in the fabric, paint, and accessories.

▶ Play with texture. Make the most of the home's original textures. That's why Steve left the front brick wall uncovered in his apartment and sandblasted paint off the flagstone fireplace in the cottage. He brings in more texture with woven fibers—sisal, raffia, and rope—all in a range of neutrals. Aged paint, worn wood, and burnished metal add texture.

▶ Mix it up. "Pieces with completely different backgrounds and provenance can still be friends," Steve says. "They may have similar lines or evoke the same feeling." In

his apartment, a 1940s leather office chair looks right at home with older English pieces.

▶ Be innovative. Use traditional or conventional elements in an unorthodox way. Steve might hang suede or leather as drapery fabric. A friend added a leather X to the white chair in the apartment's den, *above center.*

▶ Create drama with scale. The size of the room and the height of the ceiling will dictate how far you can go with scale, *opposite.* "In an open setting, a giant basket, a vase of branches, or a large framed artwork can be magnificent."

▶ Edit. "Often the room that 'needs something,' needs something taken out," he says. The well-placed look he loves takes discipline. "Use less and focus on better, more individual pieces." An oversize lantern in his cottage serves as a dramatic focal point, *above right.*

SIMPLE BED LINENS

BRANCHES AND FLOWERS

▶UNIQUE OBJECTS. Steve loves to hunt for unusual objects. He admits that most of the pieces in his homes are vintage, but says you can find great new pieces for a little more money. Some of his favorite objects include walking sticks and old canes propped against or hung on a wall, a 1920s English botanist's table next to his town sofa, and a roll of green military braid he used in the bedrooom in his apartment.

▶ONE OR TWO REALLY GOOD PIECES. Although good design exists at all price levels, Steve says that better pieces will make everything in the room look more expensive. He points to the chandelier in his apartment breakfast room and the framed flag in his cottage as really good pieces that add high style to his rooms.

▶LUMINOUS FABRICS. Beautiful fabrics add style to pillows and small stools. "I use horsehair, camelhair, cashmere, and suede—something tactile and sumptuous," he says. It's a splurge that's affordable if you only have to buy a yard or two of expensive fabric for a small project.

▶SOLID BED LINENS. Steve prefers the look of all-white for the bed. This makes it easy to add color with a throw or pillow and to change colors with the seasons.

▶CLEAR GLASS VASES. "Simple clear glass vases make anything fresh-cut come alive," he says. He loves to see the stems and the water through the glass.

▶BRANCHES AND FLOWERS. Steve is more apt to use flowers in the apartment, blooms such as roses and lilies. In the country he opts for birch branches and cut stems such as horsetail or hydrangea.

▶CANDLE CHANDELIERS. Candle chandeliers work perfectly to provide soft light in both places. He often pairs recessed lighting with chandeliers so he can adjust the lighting to the perfect setting.

PATINA

REALLY GOOD PIECES

▶THE 40-WATT LIGHTBULB. "It's about as bright as a lamp gets at my house," he says. He also loves to use 15-watt appliance bulbs for lighting.

▶FRAMES WITH EXAGGERATED MATS. "A wide mat really brings the eye into the image that it frames," Steve says. He used wide mats on the botanical prints in the apartment's den and on old maps and a Matisse sketch in the bedroom.

▶PATINA. Steve favors aged paint, worn wood, and burnished metals for the warmth and character they add. Even old paper yields a wonderful patina.

BUSINESS BASICS Seven years ago Steve Knollenberg made a huge career leap. He left the family insurance business behind and started working for an interior designer whose work he respected. Recently he decided to launch his own design firm, Stephen Knollenberg, Inc.

He designs both contemporary and traditional interiors. "I like projects where the client is open to experimentation," he says. His work includes everything from new homes to New York City apartments.

He recommends a slow and thoughtful approach. "Good rooms evolve. Take your time to find the right piece for a space or leave it blank."

STEPHEN KNOLLENBERG, INC.
ADDRESS 327 Southfield Road
Birmingham, Michigan 48009
PHONE 248/895-4455

Ford Boyd Bailey
interior designer

Ford Boyd Interiors and Verve

interior design and home furnishings shop

COLUMBIA, SOUTH CAROLINA

southern with a twist

Above: *Vintage fabric made into a pillow offers a focal point in the master bedroom. Ford Boyd Bailey's husband built the bed.*

Opposite: *Comfort is the underlying focus of Ford's decorating. She uses high cocktail tables and movable hassocks that offer extra seating.*

southern

southern style plays a big role in Ford Boyd Bailey's design work. Born and raised in the South, she appreciates its traditions. It's just that when it comes to decorating her own home or ones for clients, she handpicks what to embrace. "My bones are traditional and practical, and I want my interiors to reflect this," Ford says, "but I don't want them to be too serious."

That means thumbs down to grandmother's stiff-backed sofa and the ubiquitous pair of ceramic dogs on the mantel. It means thumbs up to Dad's leather chair and ottoman. "He sat in that chair every night to read his mail and the newspaper," Ford says.

Just don't expect her to keep the chair and ottoman together. The ottoman now occupies a place of honor in the master bedroom,

Above: *Ford designed the evening room with a warm, club feeling. During a trip to Ireland she and her husband ate in a similar library and wanted to create their own version in their home. "Everyone's drawn to that room," she says.*

Opposite: *The hammered-metal fireplace surround came from England, and they built the fireplace to fit. Ford spent two years looking for the perfect chairs, then shortened the table's legs by 4 inches to make it work with the chairs.*

while the chair sits by the secretary in the living room. After all, Ford loves to take the traditional elements of her Southern heritage and shake them up. It's a look she calls "edgy traditional." She might hang a piece of modern art low on the wall or snuggle a sofa up to a coffee table that's almost as tall as a dining table. She never puts a mantel over a fireplace. She sets a table with fine china and silver, all resting on inexpensive straw placemats. Yards and yards of beautiful silk taffeta cover the windows, but there's not a swag in sight. Garden busts inherited from her grandfather flank the front door—on the interior side.

Ford put her design philosophy to the test at home. She built a new Tuscan manor to look like a house that's been lived in and loved through several generations of a family. To create this look, Ford focused on bringing in patina with a careful mix of materials. Old beams in the entry, plaster finishes on walls, rough limestone floors, and plank ceilings and walls blur age lines. Antique architectural pieces also add to the illusion of an old house.

Once construction was finished, the house offered a backdrop for Ford's design. A rich palette of corn silk and paprika wraps rooms with warmth. One-of-a-kind pieces—artwork, chandeliers, and accessories gathered on travels—let Ford write her own history of Southern decorating, one that offers a twist on tradition. "Whether it's the arrangement of furnishings and objects or the way artwork is hung, there is always an element of surprise," she says.

Below left: *The kitchen table serves as a buffet when the chairs are pulled away. Ford uses palm fronds as a table cover.*
Below right: *The same table offers a family gathering spot for meals. The fireplace hearth sits at table height.*
Opposite: *Rough limestone floors and rustic ceiling beams age this new foyer. Ford wired candle lanterns, probably from Syria. An old architectural piece adds height above the vintage doors leading to the kitchen. A painting hung low below the mirror adds surprise.*

FORD BOYD BAILEY

Elegant fabrics and traditional furniture relaxed for today's Southern lifestyles

▶ Create an ageless background. Ford used limestone floors, stucco walls, old beams, plank ceilings and walls, and masonry fireplaces to hide the fact that her home is just three years old, *opposite*.

▶ Plan for comfort. "When I was brought up, we weren't allowed to go into the living room," Ford says. Now she fills every room in the house, including the living room, with comfortable furniture. She likes to place furniture so it

encourages conversations for groups of three. "If you have twelve people in a room," she says, "they're not talking to everyone at once." If you're building a new home, make sure the rooms are large enough for company yet intimate for family nights at home.

▶ Pick a warm color scheme for a new home. The color scheme for Ford's house came from a beautiful embroidered satin altar cloth she found in England. "The luscious paprika red became the red thread throughout," Ford says.

▶ Select neutral solid-color fabrics for upholstery, such as linen and cotton velvet, suede, and imitation suede, *above right*. Ford likes to use washable cotton canvas for summer slipcovers.

▶ Hang window treatments. She loves to create traditional panels using yards and

yards of sumptuous fabrics, *above center*. Blinds keep the look tailored and adaptable from night to day. Window treatments can quickly change a room's mood. Ford visited a client who wanted to redo her room. Instead Ford "fixed" the room with window treatments.

▶ Don't overfill the spaces. She likes the clean look of furniture with breathing space around it and a few accessories on a tabletop. She hangs artwork with white space around it. "I hang it so you look at the art," she says.

▶ Add lighting. Stay away from recessed lights and direct overhead lighting, if possible. She prefers the soft glow of lamps, chandeliers, and sconces.

▶ Mix old and new. Ford combines new and old accessories and furniture to give her home a collected-over-time look.

PRETTY PILLOWS

HANDMADE RUGS

▶**PRETTY PILLOWS.** Ford uses elegant fabrics and trim or vintage pieces to make one-of-a-kind pillows. But she cautions, use only a few pillows on a sofa or you won't leave room for sitting. "Make sure your furniture says 'come relax,' not 'go away,'" Ford says.

▶**WOVEN GRASS RUGS.** Sea-grass rugs are great while you're saving up to buy an expensive rug. But they're also fun to use with more formal furnishings and fabrics. "They can instantly relax a room," Ford says.

▶**GOOD ART.** Ford often picks up new pieces of art on her travels. "It is an important investment," she says. She likes to mix modern art with vintage paintings and Italian engravings.

▶**PALM FRONDS.** Instead of flowers Ford uses palm fronds and grasses, either alone in a vase or clustered for a centerpiece. "I love the evocative feeling of the way fronds and grasses blow in the breeze," she says. These plants have an added bonus: They last a long time once cut. She also lays palm fronds as a "tablecloth" on the buffet table.

▶**IRON.** Iron offers instant patina when used in lamps, sconces, chandeliers, and candlestands. She mixes old and new iron throughout her house. The chandelier in the evening room (see page 102) is an old Italian candle chandelier that she electrified.

▶**OTTOMANS OR HASSOCKS.** She buys ottomans or hassocks 20 inches high so they're the same seat height as a chair. "I use a lot of hassocks because you can pull them around," she says. In the living room hassocks add enough seating to make room for 14 people.

▶**TARNISHED SILVER AND BRASS.** "You're more apt to use it if it's tarnished," Ford says, explaining that if you keep these metals polished you'll probably leave them in the cupboard.

▶**PIECES FROM OTHER CULTURES.** Ford collects small tables and mirrors from Morocco or Mexico. "They're so unique," she says. "They give a room a little twist." She likes the way they start a new tradition.

▶**HANDMADE RUGS.** Ford is slowly acquiring handmade rugs for her home. As

IRON

PALM FRONDS

VINTAGE FABRICS

SPECIALIZED STORAGE

her collection grows, it replaces the grass rugs. "I love beautiful rugs, but they're expensive," she says. She suggests buying a smaller handmade rug and laying it on top of a sea-grass rug. When you can afford a larger rug, move the small rug to a hallway, bathroom, or entry.

▶SPECIALIZED STORAGE. Ford entertains often and likes to share the evening room with guests. The armoire in the room, customized by her husband, offers space for lots of bar gear.

▶VINTAGE FABRICS. An embroidered satin altar cloth Ford found in England became a valance in the evening room. It took her a year to find the pumpkin color velvet to complement the vintage piece.

BUSINESS BASICS
When Ford started her interior design business in 1984, she didn't plan on owning a shop as well. It's just that her clients needed a place closer to home where they could find the right pieces. So Ford opened Verve, *above*, and filled it with art, furniture, and accessories.

VERVE
ADDRESS 1127 Gregg Street
Columbia, South Carolina 29201
PHONE 803/799-0045

FORD BOYD INTERIORS
ADDRESS 1127 Gregg Street,
Columbia, South Carolina 29201
PHONE 803/254-9953
WEBSITE www.verveinteriors.com
E-MAIL info@verveinteriors.com

> *"I love talking to people. I still like to pop into the stores and see how things are going."*
>
> —KIRK SCHLUPP, MIG AND TIG

shopkeepers

Bitten by the retail bug, these hardworking style entrepreneurs aren't your average shopkeepers. Designers and artists first, they know that great design makes good business sense. Step into one of their shops and you'll see the difference immediately. These are the shops you love to visit again and again for their inspiring ideas and handpicked objects to take home. For them, style doesn't stay behind the shop doors. Here's how they transform the look they love at retail into the look they live with at home.

> *"I love the fact you never know who's going to walk through the door, who you're going to meet, and what they're going to want."*
>
> —CINDI GAETKE, ELLINGTON

"We try to keep the shop looking like a staged set."
—MADELINE ROTH, PARISCOPE

"I feel like I do art in my work every day. I treat Clutter as an art show for me, as an installation."
—D'ETTE COLE, CLUTTER AND UNCOMMON OBJECTS

"Everything is handpicked by us, either in Europe or in the U.S., but our personal stamp of approval is on it."
—CAROLINE VERSCHOOR, EKSTER

"We're retailers. We love the energy and the challenge of it. Just think how great it is to go into a wonderful store."
—PAUL SCHNEIDER, TWIST

Madeline Roth

shopkeeper

Pariscope

vintage and new objects with French attitude

GENEVA, ILLINOIS

french lessons

Madeline Roth makes a bold style statement in her living room with pink walls, painted checked floors, and a surprising mix of furniture.
Opposite: She uses her collection of vintage poodle dishes every day.

THE JOYS OF WINE

Left: *Instead of remodeling the kitchen, Madeline retained the butler's pantry (not shown), repainted the existing metal cabinets her favorite shade of pink, and covered the floor with diagonally-placed vinyl tiles. The range is vintage. Vinyl kitchen chairs, dating from the 1940s, showcase her favorite design decade.*
Opposite: *A French pier mirror reflects the living room. Madeline removed the wiring from the French chandelier and outfitted it with candles.*

Francophile

Madeline Roth might slip a tape of *Top Hat* into the VCR, but it's not because she's pining to see Fred Astaire and Ginger Rogers dancing cheek to cheek. No, this shopkeeper is checking out the decorating. "The interiors in that film are just wonderful," she says of the 1935 movie.

Madeline loves old American magazines as well, especially those from the '20s, '30s, and '40s. She studies their pages for inspiration. "I particularly like what was done in the forties," she says. It was wartime and that meant people were making do—painting old furniture instead of buying new, for example.

Children's books from the 1930s and 1940s are another source of decorating inspiration. Madeline admits that's where she sometimes finds the perfect color scheme for a room or a fun decorative flourish. Books recounting the adventures of the red-haired Parisian, Madeline, are among her favorites. So it's no surprise that Madeline Roth's shop, Pariscope, in Geneva, Illinois, and her 1920s home are filled with French objects from the first half of the 1900s.

When she and her husband bought the vintage house, it was dated but in good shape. They made mostly cosmetic changes, opting to keep the existing kitchen and living room cabinetry. To create the right setting for her look, Madeline tore down heavy draperies and opened up windows, brushed overscale diagonal checks on floors, and lightened walls with shades of pink.

Her decorating style draws from the aesthetic foundations of the French—their love for antiquities, their witty use of eclectic pieces, and their elevation of ordinary objects to treasure status. "The French make do with things we probably wouldn't," she says. They might throw a beautiful vintage dress over a tattered chair or wrap a bureau with rope. "They do things that are very unexpected."

So does Madeline. In her living room, she hangs clusters of millinery bananas from a lampshade rim and covers her fireplace opening with part of a stage set. Playing with pieces and getting them right suits Madeline perfectly. "I consider myself more of a stylist than a decorator."

Above: Madeline was told that the living room cases came from a Portuguese apothecary and were added to the house in the 1940s. She adapted a marble floor design she saw in a photo of a vintage hotel lobby in England and painted it on the foyer floor.

Opposite: The dining room set dates from the 1910s. Madeline found it in Florida and re-covered the seats. She uses a French armoire for dishes. "You don't have to have a buffet," she says. The shutters are original to the house.

Although she spent 14 years as a contractor building new homes in the Chicago suburbs, Madeline likes this switch to shopkeeper and stylist. It fulfills her passion for antiques, visual display, and interior design.

When she opened her store in 1995, the idea was to re-create the wildly unusual displays from Paris flea markets and provide a diverse inventory of French antiques. Eight years later she has a larger building, offers a collection of French antiques, and sells a smattering of new books, hatboxes, and T-shirts. She also holds an annual Paris Flea Market each June.

"The shop is always in a state of change, but I like to keep my house stable," she says. That's really not much of a problem, though. "I have my house looking really the way I want."

Madeline likes to add her own special touches, such as the milliner's fruit on the lampshade and ticking trim on the French chaise. She bought the 1910 self-portrait in Wisconsin. She was told that the painter studied in Paris. "I would never give it up," she says.

Opposite: Seating arrangements cluster about the living room. Upholstered pieces gather to make room for groups of two or more. Madeline likes to use small tables and stools because they can be moved to wherever they're needed.

GET THE LOOK

MADELINE ROTH

A playful approach using 20th-century French and French-inspired antiques in a 1920s house

▶ Use two colors plus white. "It's a relatively simple way to have a beautiful room," she says. She finds a color she likes, such as her new pick, a "wonderful turquoise blue." Then she mixes it with one other color per room. She uses her favorite pink the same way, *above center*. "I think of pink as a neutral color. It goes with black, brown, gray, and blue."

▶ Make it beautiful. "Beauty is what my look is all about," Madeline says. She may create it with a wonderful color, layers of pretty objects, or details on a pillow. "It's important to be surrounded by beauty even if it's just in a tiny little room."

▶ Add whimsy and humor. "It is the most important ingredient in design," she says. "Don't take your surroundings too seriously." She hung milliner's fruit from a lampshade rim, *above right*. Kitchen shade pulls are white plastic. "They look like charms from Cracker Jack boxes."

▶ Paint the floors. "I like floors painted in the two contrasting colors in a room's color scheme," she says. She uses oversize checks in the living room painted on the diagonal, *opposite*.

▶ Add hand-painted elements on walls, ceilings, and furniture. They can be as complicated as the "tented" ceiling in the kitchen or as refined as the deep pink

circles and ovals painted to show off the intaglios above the fireplace mantel. (See page 113.)

▶ Use small-pattern fabrics. People tend to tire of large floral patterns. "Checks, stripes, dots, and little geometrics are timeless," she says.

▶ Introduce scallops. They're everywhere in Madeline's home, circling the kitchen table, bridging the kitchen alcove, and hugging the edges of a table.

▶ Take your time. "My look is an undecorated look, as though the rooms evolved over the years," she says.

▶ Edit, edit, edit. Madeline admits that it requires discipline to keep a home as spare as hers. "Because my decorating is more streamlined, each piece becomes important," she says.

BIG OBJECTS

COLLECTIONS

▶BARE WINDOWS. Unless you have a privacy problem, keep the windows bare. "I like seeing the windows and the mullions," she says. "I like seeing out." If you have to use a window covering for privacy or sun control, use simple shades.

▶MIRRORS. Whether they're bigger than an armoire or hold-in-your-hand small, mirrors add a bit of sparkle to Madeline's interiors. A French pier mirror anchors one end of the living room. A cluster of small mirrors decorates a wall in the hall.

▶BIG OBJECTS. Large objects offer a surprise. Oversize painted boxwood topiaries, an Irish case clock, and an oversize floor pattern define the foyer.

▶VINTAGE TABLEWARE. Madeline collects 1950s-era poodle dishes by Glidden and restaurantware featuring turquoise polka dots. She uses these dishes rather than new ones for everyday meals.

▶COLLECTIONS. When Madeline found a group of porcelain intaglios in Paris, she had to have them. At first she considered framing them, but "they looked way too serious for the room," she says. So she improvised, popping off their paper backing, then using double-stick tape to attach each intaglio to the wall in an intricate pattern. "If you have something you like, you can make it work," she says. Madeline also hung nine watercolors of costumed women in her living room windows, one framed painting per window. "I really loved them and there really wasn't another place to use them." (See the reflection on page 118.)

▶CHANDELIERS AND LAMPS. Both lighting sources make multiple appearances in Madeline's home. She buys vintage pieces, mostly French and from the 1930s or 1940s. The chandelier in the dining room is Venetian glass. The candle chandelier over the daybed is wood covered with gilt. Madeline removed the wiring and added candles to this French piece.

▶OTTOMANS AND STOOLS. Madeline found three little stools with black seats in France. "They don't match, but they were all together when I found them." Now she uses them as extra seating in the living room. When she bought the green ottoman in front of the fireplace (see page 113), it was covered in threadbare gold fabric. She reupholstered it exactly the way it was covered originally.

▶SMALL TABLES. Small tables with decorative bases give Madeline the flexibility to move them where they're needed. She loves fanciful bases such as the table in the living room that looks like it's made from old musical instruments (see page 119).

▶FLOWERS. Madeline likes pink roses, of course. But she loves to make arrangements that also stand out, so she masses different colors of roses in a single vase—orange, red, pink, and yellow.

BUSINESS BASICS
Madeline shops in France to fill her store, Pariscope—but not at flea markets in Paris. Instead she shops the countryside looking for pieces to bring home. Other items, obviously inspired by the French look, come from this country. "We're going for a look," she says.

She fills her shop with things from the turn of the 20th century to the 1950s and new dishes, books, and fabrics. Special events include a Paris Flea Market in June and a lavender festival in September.

PARISCOPE
ADDRESS 22 N. 3rd Street
Geneva, Illinois 60134
PHONE 630/232-1600
WEBSITE www.pariscope.net

Cindi Gaetke
shopkeeper

Ellington

clothing and home furnishings

CHARLESTON, SOUTH CAROLINA

living above the shop

Cindi Gaetke loves Art Deco furnishings for their glamour. She sells them in her store and uses them in her apartment. **Opposite:** Cindi combines clothing and home furnishings at the store's entrance as an introduction to the unusual mix that waits inside.

fashion

fashion or furniture store? Cindi Gaetke didn't intend to sell armoires in her Charleston clothing store. "I had beautiful garment racks designed for the store. I purchased handmade Chinese armoires and tables for display," she says. Customers soon wanted more than just the clothes off the racks, however. They wanted the store's display furniture too.

So Cindi did what any wise shopkeeper would do. She expanded into home furnishings. The move also opened up a whole new venue for her design talents. "The first sale started my career in interior design," she says. Customers wanted to know where to place the new furniture. Now she's just as apt to advise a customer about getting the perfect hand-painted duvet for the bed as in pairing the right shirt and pants.

Tending a retail shop isn't new for Cindi. Once she turned 14, she spent every day after school and every weekend working in her parents' outfitters' department store in a small South Carolina town. The family business sold everything from bed linens to coats, shirts, and pants for the entire family.

Retail is still the best job for her. "I love the fact you never know who's going to walk through the door, who you're going to meet, and what they're going to want," she says. And like her parents before her, she lives close to the work she loves.

Left: *In the master bedroom, Cindi added a bench opposite the front window. The mix of modern and Asian reflects the pieces she sells in her downstairs shop.*
Opposite: *In the shop, items for the home mix with clothing. Cindi likes to set everything against warm, neutral backdrops. It creates a look that feels welcoming. "I like to mix it up a lot," she says.*

"My parents lived above their store when they were first married," she says. "That was pre-me, but I always heard stories about how much they enjoyed it."

It's no surprise that when presented with the same opportunity, Cindi moved in above the shop. Now when she turns the lock in the shop door each night, she walks up the staircase to her second-floor apartment.

The living arrangement may seem unusual, but, for Cindi, it feels perfectly wonderful. She loves the in-town location of her home and shop in a two-story Charleston single house. And she finds the small space perfect for the way she and her husband want to live.

The look of the shop and home are purely Cindi. For both upstairs and downstairs she started with a palette of soft colors. Then she added one-of-a-kind Art Deco, modern, and Chinese furniture pieces, and layered on elegance with accessories such as hand-painted silk duvets and beaded sconces. "All of these things invoke vintage glamour," she says.

It may seem like a long way from a rural outfitters' department store to a sophisticated urban boutique, but Cindi puts it all in perspective. Customers, after all, are looking for the same things from the shopkeeper, no matter where they shop, Cindi says. They want a good listener who gives them good service.

A hand-painted silk duvet topped by an antique silk sari adds luxury to the master bedroom. Cindi likes to create an elegant look with beautiful fabrics such as the 15-inch-wide hand-painted scarf hanging over the fireplace. "I love doing things like that with pieces you can wear or hang," she says.

CINDI GAETKE

Casual contemporary elegance with an Asian twist

▸ Choose wall colors that flow from room to room. Cindi uses soft natural colors, including browns, greens, terra-cotta, and gray blues. When you pick your colors, think about the ceilings, too, which should be painted a lighter tone of the wall color. Replacing white or cream on the walls with color really makes a difference. "It makes any house look more expensive," she says.

▸ Make rooms work for the way you want to live. Cindi turned the largest room in her apartment into the master bedroom.

She's away at work for long hours so the bedroom is the place that offers her the most sanctuary at night. The rest of the apartment includes a small den, a music room, *above center,* a dining room, and an office. The kitchen downstairs is a leftover from the building's days as a restaurant. That's fine with Cindi, who doesn't cook much.

▸ Select comfortable furniture. Cindi's customers want to dress comfortably and they want their homes to be comfortable. She suggests buying upholstered furniture with a down/feather mix. "This will give fabulous comfort without having to purchase overstuffed, massive upholstered pieces," she says.

▸ Do something totally unexpected. For Cindi that might mean painting one wall a contrasting color, adding a funky Art Deco lamp to a room with classic

furnishings, or using a scarf as wall art. "Just add a surprise," she says.

▸ Add an abundance of texture. "Texture will increase the depth and lushness of your surroundings." she says. She uses fabrics such as a nubby cotton or sleek silk, and she loves velvet.

▸ Keep it spare. "Don't overdo," Cindi says. "Less is truly best." A few good pieces of furniture will carry a room. And having fewer pieces makes it easier to move furniture to change the focal point seasonally from a fireplace to a window.

▸ Mix it up. Cindi advises against using furniture exclusively from a certain design period. "The key to making this work is picking classic designs you will never tire of," she says. She loves the mix of Art Deco, 1850s Chinese, and clean-lined contemporary.

FLOWERS

ART DECO PIECES

▶**INTERESTING RUGS.** Cindi uses rugs throughout to add texture. She likes Turkish rugs and those with an Art Deco twist. She also uses rugs that look like sisal.

▶**HAND-PAINTED SILK.** Silk duvets, pillows, and scarves all get a one-of-a-kind look with hand painting. Cindi works with a local designer to create her ideas.

▶**ART DECO PIECES.** It could be a wonderful lamp or a great piece of furniture.

"Mixed with traditional or contemporary pieces, it always makes a statement."

▶**LAMPS.** "They're the perfect accessory," Cindi says. She uses them to accent artwork, as well as to warm up a room, and mixes sconces with floor and table lamps.

▶**OTTOMANS.** She groups several as a coffee table or uses them singly for extra seating. She prefers cubes because they are the most versatile shape.

▶**ROMAN SHADES.** Cindi prefers simple window treatments. "The fabric itself should make the statement," she says. "Keep the design simple and timeless."

▶**THROWS.** She uses them for texture and style, like the vintage sari on the bed.

▶**FLOWERS.** Cindi keeps flowers in her bedroom, especially calla lilies when they're in season. "It makes you feel good when you wake up and see them," she says.

BUSINESS BASICS Jazz, fashion, and home furnishings. It's all part of the mix at Cindi Gaetke's shop called Ellington. The store, named after jazz musician Duke Ellington, regularly hosts jazz groups. It's also where Cindi sells her handpicked selection of fashion and home furnishings, everything from fabric lines not available in Charleston to antique saris that she uses for custom window coverings and bed throws. An assortment of Art Deco and Asian furniture expands the shop's offerings.

Cindi buys, too, from up-and-coming clothing designers. "I don't want anything that you can find anywhere else nearby, hopefully not within the state," she says. To stay fresh she has to keep finding new designers and ordering new pieces.

ELLINGTON
ADDRESS 82 Society Street, Charleston, South Carolina 29401 **PHONE** 843/722-7999

objects of their affection

Paul Schneider and Lauren Eulau

shopkeepers

Twist

contemporary studio crafts galleries

PORTLAND, OREGON ❦ SEATTLE, WASHINGTON

Paul Schneider and Lauren Eulau use
strong but subdued wall colors and
simply shaped furniture as a perfect
backdrop for colorful art.
Opposite: Functional art pieces, such as
vases and dishes, don't always have to
be in use. Paul also likes to display them.

Black frames unite artwork above the credenza. Paul and Lauren use repeating elements like this to make a style statement.
Opposite: *By removing walls in their 1930s home, Paul and Lauren opened up the space. Bigger windows also let in more light. Although they display their art collection on tabletops, windowsills, and walls, the rooms still feel lived-in and welcoming.*

artists

Paul Schneider and his wife, Lauren Eulau, have always been crazy about art, creating their own works of art and buying objects made by others. But not just any objects. At a time when their rent was $140 a month, they spent $260 for a handmade ceramic vase by a favorite potter. Now some 30 years later, they still buy contemporary studio crafts—for their own home and for the three galleries, called Twist, that they own in Portland, Oregon, and Seattle.

"Some people pay a huge amount for a car or a vacation," says Paul. "We buy art."

They know their subject well. Lauren, a weaver, and Paul, a potter, met in art school and both worked their crafts for years, selling their pieces at an artists' cooperative and at Saturday markets. But their passion for art took a surprising turn. They found they loved the business of selling contemporary handmade pieces more than the craft of making them. "We love the energy and the challenge of retail. It's so complicated, and it's so exciting to make it work. Just think how wonderful it is to go into a great store," says Paul.

So Paul and Lauren left their crafts-making behind and focused solely on building their gallery business. Now they sell beautiful handmade objects, all made in small studios by trained artists whom they know. "We buy for the store, but if we didn't love it enough to also take it home, we wouldn't buy it," says Paul.

Above left: Colorful objects pop against the living room's white fireplace. Deep burgundy walls copy the colors of upholstery in the adjacent sitting room.
Below left: A calmer palette rules in the upstairs bedroom. The one-of-a-kind blanket chest at the foot of the bed combines wood carving and painting.
Opposite: Bookcases with movable shelves serve as showcases for single objects; halogen lights add drama to items placed on top. The windowsills are also deep enough to hold art objects.

So it's no surprise that their home is filled with the same wonderful objects on display in their galleries. What is surprising is that their 1930s home looks typical on the outside with its centered door, symmetrical windows, and wood siding. Inside, however, this artistic pair removed walls and added windows to create a light, open space for their collections. They built bookcases and added deep windowsills as display spaces for objects they love to collect. They also brought in lighting that focuses on special art pieces while still creating a comfortable living space.

Then the couple added color—lots of color, a jumble of color. It swathes walls in burgundy and sage green, covers upholstery in olive and red stripes, and most of all, shows up in their collection of art objects in hues from sultry yellow to hot pink.

Their art is the ever-changing element. When they bring home a new piece, they rotate another piece to a wall of storage they built in their basement. "We're buying for ourselves constantly," says Paul. And, of course, loving each new purchase.

"Some collectors like us never say no. They never have enough," says Paul, with a laugh. "We need those kind of people."

LAUREN EULAU AND
PAUL SCHNEIDER

Studio-made crafts
for display and
use in a 1930s house
updated with open
spaces and color

▶ Be fearless with color. "Colorful objects look better in the context of rich colors," says Paul. He and Lauren use bold colors on the main floor, changing color from room to room, and softer, calmer hues in their second-floor bedrooms.

▶ Put a handmade object on its own "pedestal." It looks more important when it's surrounded by space, such as one piece of glass on a shelf or a platter hung on the kitchen wall, *above center*.

▶ Appreciate the rhythm of combining objects in like shapes, materials, or colors. Consider the impact of a small cabinet full of skull cups or a mantel half-filled with acrylic candlesticks. Don't buy for repetition. Buy what you love. If a theme develops, that just reflects your taste.

▶ Create spaces for collections. They built deep windowsills and divided bookcases to hold collections. They added generalized display spaces that fit different objects of a similar scale. Movable shelves allow them to adjust the space as their collections change.

▶ Illuminate art objects. "It's hugely important," Paul says. "Embrace darkness and don't light everything." The relationship between light and dark is what makes the whole effect work. "I like lighting that makes you want to sit down," says Paul, who prefers most of

the glow on the lower part of the room. For drama he spotlights specific objects with just one bulb.

▶ Use natural light. When they remodeled their home, they added lots of south-facing windows and left them uncovered.

▶ Add art to the kitchen, *opposite,* and bath. Put something there to look at since you spend lots of time in those rooms.

▶ Buy only the pieces you're passionate about. Don't buy something just to fill a specific space.

▶ Play with symmetry. Match objects with similar scale and shape but not exact copies. Similar lamps on either end of the sofa offer symmetry with a twist.

▶ Seek design help. An architect designed their kitchen, *above right.*

GOOD ART

FUNCTIONAL ART

FUNCTIONAL ART

WHIMSICAL ART

▶GOOD ART. Don't make do, says Paul. Buy what you're passionate about, even if it means saving for a while or putting something on layaway.

▶WHIMSICAL ART. A Ferris wheel on the living room mantel offers the color, whimsy, and "folkiness" they prefer.

▶FUNCTIONAL ART. Objects such as mouth-blown drinking glasses, handmade platters, tables, and lamps are art you can use. Artful objects hold wooden spoons,

snacks, flowers, and more. Paul loves to display these functional pieces.

▶THREE-DIMENSIONAL ART. It's easier to fill a large wall space, such as the area over a mantel or above the range, with a three-dimensional object such as a platter or a bowl. The wall space becomes a "frame" for the art object.

▶AFFORDABLE ART. Skull cups stored on a custom shelf are one of Paul's favorite collections. They cost just $35 each.

▶HANDCRAFTED FURNITURE. If you see a piece of furniture you like, ask about it. Most artisans will take custom orders.

▶GRAPHIC FRAMES. Let the art speak. On their dining room wall, Paul and Lauren framed all the artwork in the same black frames.

▶CUSTOM DISPLAY. Movable shelves make room for favorite large pieces.

▶BARE WINDOWS. Use window treatments only where you need privacy.

AFFORDABLE ART

CUSTOM DISPLAY

BUSINESS BASICS At their Twist galleries, Paul Schneider and Lauren Eulau sell contemporary studio-made pieces crafted by trained artisans. Former artists, they love creating retail spaces more than making the objects. "The marketplace has gotten a lot more sophisticated," Paul says. And so have the objects. Each piece they sell has a twist that makes it unique.

TWIST (PORTLAND, OREGON)
ADDRESS 30 NW 23rd Place
PHONE 503/224-0334

ADDRESS 700 SW 5th Avenue
PHONE 503/222-3137

TWIST (SEATTLE, WASHINGTON)
ADDRESS 600 Pine Street
PHONE 206/315-8080
WEBSITE www.twistonline.com

the **Curiosity** *shopper*

D'Ette Cole

shopkeeper

Uncommon Objects,
AUSTIN, TEXAS

Clutter,
WARRENTON, TEXAS

D'Ette Cole created a headboard by stacking three hollow-core doors. New and vintage linens dress the bed. The photo collage is her own work.
Opposite: A modern dressing table holds jewelry sorted by color on bowling trophies and a cakestand. The 1940s chair mixes toile with "cha-cha" fringe.

give

give D'Ette Cole a box of odds and ends pulled from an attic and she'll sift through the contents until her hands blacken with grit and grime. When she comes up for air, she's apt to have accumulated a small pile of keepers, the flotsam and jetsam from someone's life. "I'm so drawn to little bits of things," she says.

She takes some of these little bits home to use for decorating or to incorporate into her artwork. Others end up for sale through Uncommon Objects, an antiques mall in Austin, Texas, and Clutter, a semiannual antiques show in Warrenton, Texas. "It's always such a treasure hunt there."

But for D'Ette, the hunt for keepers doesn't stop with the small stuff. She collects a wide range of objects, from small to much, much larger than a breadbox. Her trove includes vintage fabrics from England and France, plastic anatomy teaching models, original art, shells and coral, lab glass, rustic farm furniture, Victorian hair art, repaired ironstone and porcelain, signs that light up, and weird plant specimens. The list goes on and on.

Her collections fill her home—a 20-year-old house with concrete floors painted blue and 24-foot-high ceilings filled with skylights. "It's a big box really," D'Ette says. But not just any ordinary box. It's a treasure house of objects, all placed for maximum effect by this former art major.

"My collections and my things give me comfort," she says. "Letting them dictate the direction I take my decor is good." That means shelves filled with objects sorted by color, fanciful and unexpected "window treatments" made from stacked paper and fabric parasols, pieces of furniture "married" for an eclectic look, architectural remnants reused inside, and a rug with Early American motifs coexisting with a flying saucer lampshade.

"I take a very unserious approach to my surroundings," she says—but not an unstudied one. D'Ette uses the design principles she learned in college to turn her home into her largest canvas. The techniques work. They give her home a comfortable human scale and create visual order from her collecting obsession.

D'ETTE COLE

Curiosities and collections in a contemporary concrete house

▶ Mix it up. D'Ette's eclectic mix includes modern and classic, rustic and dressy, handmade and machine-made. "I like taking things from different styles and periods, and combining and customizing them to make them my own," she says.

▶ Add bold color. "Strong color transforms and defines spaces," she says. Her current favorites include reds (tomato, bright red, orange red, and coral), black (gloss and chalky), lavender, periwinkle blue, and shades of pink. D'Ette even used

black paint in her tiny kitchen. "It adds some sophistication to my otherwise bachelor-pad kitchen," she says.

▶ Use pattern and texture sparingly. A wall of books can add this effect. So can a wall filled with framed mirrors. In her bedroom she used vintage toile with checks. "I don't like too many competing patterns," she says. "It's too confusing." Even her five spotted dogs fit. "I love dogs with pattern on them," she says.

▶ Play with scale. "You need contrast from tiny to small to big to really big," she says. If everything is the same size, nothing stands out. She applies this concept to the objects she places on a bathroom shelf, *opposite*. "It gives a sense of order and balance," she says.

▶ Incorporate architectural antiques. She loves them for the rich texture of their

weathered surfaces and for their over-the-top scale. "Architectural pieces reference places that no longer exist. They remind me of places and spaces I've been to in my life that don't exist anymore," she says.

▶ Hang chandeliers. To this artist they look like mobiles hanging from the ceiling. In the past year, she added chandeliers to her kitchen and by her bed, *above right*.

▶ Include elements of surprise. An oversize fishing hook restrains a curtain, a knobby walking stick becomes a curtain rod, and a cakestand holds shells, *above center*. "It's what I call re-purposing," she says.

▶ Buy a new, comfortable sofa. D'Ette likes an overstuffed sofa with simple lines and in a neutral color. "If I want to mix it up, I can always drape it with an old French quilt or a Persian textile," she says.

BIG SCALE

BITS AND PIECES

▶**BITS AND PIECES.** "I'm always looking at the ground and finding bits here and there," she says. The piece that draws her eye might be a printed fortune carelessly dropped, a beautiful shell washed up on the beach, or a squashed piece of metal in an interesting shape. "I like including random things in my home," she says. They might find their way to a shelf in her curiosity cabinet, to a bowl, or to the assemblage artwork she makes.

▶**FAMILY PHOTOS.** To create impact D'Ette groups her family photographs on one wall. "I never tire of looking at these framed faces," she says. "They comfort and ground me and remind me where I came from."

▶**SPARKLY THINGS.** "I'm like a crow that way," she says. "I've always been attracted to shiny, sparkly things." D'Ette uses mirrors and mirrored objects for their ability to extend space. She has a collection of mirrored disco balls in various sizes and patterns, an old mirrored garden ball, and a group of Moravian stars in different sizes and glass patterns. Sometimes she even slips a sparkly rhinestone pin into a still life of shells.

▶**FRENCH LINEN SHEETS.** D'Ette may use a sheet as a bed cover or turn a pair into long curtain panels. "I sew on those big old wooden curtain rings and put them on a piece of dried bamboo for a rod. It looks very casual," she says. For a no-sew idea,

she lays the sheet across the bed, placing the monogram so that it shows between the bed skirt and the duvet.

▶**ENGLISH TRANSFERWARE.** "I like the patterns, colors, and look of the old English transferware dishes," she says. A favorite piece holds toothpaste and a toothbrush on a bathroom shelf. She likes the way transferware blends with vintage French textiles.

▶**FRENCH TEXTILES.** D'Ette buys her 19th-century French florals, stripes, and toiles in red or black and uses large pieces for window and bed coverings and smaller pieces for cushions and pillows. "The dyes have this vibrancy that you just don't see

in new fabrics," she says. D'Ette finds her French pieces mainly in Provence. She goes to a couple of antiques fairs there, but buys mostly from small town markets.

▶BIG SCALE. She suggests using objects bigger than a bread box. No, says D'Ette, make that a television set. But the sofa and ottoman don't count. She uses decorative chests, architectural pieces, and even light fixtures to add drama. D'Ette loves a pair of oversize urns she placed on top of a cabinet that separates the sitting and dining areas in her home. The urns were crafted from old tires that have been stitched together and painted to look like terra-cotta.

BUSINESS BASICS D'Ette Cole sells antiques at Uncommon Objects, an antiques mall in Austin, Texas, and Clutter, a semiannual antiques show in Warrenton, Texas. Her business, Etta Industry, offers residential interior design.

ETTA INDUSTRY
PHONE 512/303-3055
WEBSITE www.ettaindustry.com

CLUTTER
ADDRESS Warrenton, Texas
PHONE 512/303-3055

UNCOMMON OBJECTS
ADDRESS 1512 S. Congress
Austin, Texas 78704
PHONE 512/442-4000

Kirk Schlupp and Vicki Semke

shopkeepers

Mig and Tig

furnishing stores with a modern outlook

CHICAGO AND WINNETKA

the softer side of **modern**

Kirk Schlupp and Vicki Semke remodeled their 1950s split-level and filled it with furnishings that reflect the house's style. They removed partial walls to open the kitchen to the dining and living rooms. **Opposite:** Kirk and Vicki prefer large pieces of art like these 6-foot-tall photographs of leaves they hung in their master bedroom.

An L-shape sofa provides lots of seating in the lower-level family room. Clean-looking plantation shutters cover the windows.
Opposite: "I like artwork that's very tongue-in-cheek," Vicki says, referring to the piece on the dining room wall. For Kirk simple graphic rugs also serve as artwork.

designers
Vicki Semke and Kirk Schlupp teamed up on their first project by happenstance. A Chicago furniture gallery dressed his custom bed with her custom bedding. They met briefly at the gallery opening. A few years later Vicki and Kirk met again, this time when Vicki hired Kirk to design an iron table for a client. Soon they were collaborating on projects. "He would make the bench," Vicki says. "I would make the cushion." The projects grew, and so did the relationship.

Ten years later, working together for this married couple is both personal and professional. They own furniture stores called Mig and Tig and a 1950s house that reflects their design partnership.

With a busy life building a business, it took Vicki and Kirk seven years to redo their 2,000-square-foot home. At first they did much of the work themselves, removing partial walls to create one large open space for the living room, dining room, and kitchen. They also gutted the kitchen and brought in maple cabinets and granite countertops that give the space a dressed-for-dinner look.

Although their style at home was simple and spare, their stores were filled to the brim. That changed two years ago after the birth of their son. Going to multiple markets and finding the "next best thing" was running them ragged. "We had to spend a week buying accessories instead of coming up with designs and ideas," Vicki says.

So Kirk and Vicki refocused their energy on their first love, furniture. They refined their look even further, creating a new name, "organic modern," to reflect the style that features reclaimed woods and soft finishes. "It's earthy and comfortable," Kirk says.

Kirk says that every so often a realtor stops by the store after hearing clients describe a home as having "a Mig and Tig look." They tell the couple they really have created an image. "We're not trying to set a trend," Vicki says. "I just want us to be Mig and Tig."

153

Art makes a bold statement in the living room. Kirk and Vicki like to keep the look neutral by using the same color of paint throughout the house. The subtly patterned upholstery fabrics wear well with a toddler in the house. **Opposite:** They use touches of leather, around the mirror and on the console, as an accent.

KIRK SCHLUPP AND
VICKI SEMKE

Organic modern colors and furniture in a 1950s modern house

▶ Complement the architecture. Because their house is a 1956 contemporary, they prefer clean-lined furnishings. The rooms are open and spare and so are the finishes, colors, and furniture. "We're all about simplicity," Kirk says.

▶ Start with a neutral background. White paint warmed with sage covers the walls. Vicki and Kirk used the same color on every wall. They like the way the color flows from room to room. "It's an earthy, organic color," Kirk says.

▶ Use medium-tone woods. The floors in Kirk and Vicki's home are light and match the tone of the wood ceilings. They used a slightly darker tone on the new maple cabinets in the kitchen.

▶ Play with scale. That includes oversize artwork that fills a wall, *opposite,* or an extra-large light fixture hanging in the dining room. It also means opting for a long sofa and big coffee table instead of using lots of pieces of furniture.

▶ Add good upholstery. Kirk and Vicki consider both comfort and style for upholstered pieces. They used muted patterns for upholstery, *above center.* Parents of a toddler, they considered the fabric's wearability. "I don't want to have sheets over the furniture," Vicki says.

▶ Incorporate touches of leather. "We do leather in bits and pieces," she says. "It's

just like a rich food. You don't want to overindulge." Leather shows up as woven strips on the living room console and as a wraparound cover on the mirror.

▶ Use rugs sparingly. "We really try to find rugs that fit the scale of the room," Vicki says. They like rugs with cleaner, tighter patterns, such as the color squares on the dining room rug. "I look at rugs almost like pieces of art," Kirk says.

▶ Install recessed lighting. Vicki and Kirk added recessed lighting when they remodeled. Now they use lamps only as accents. "For this style of house, the lighting has to be cleaner," Vicki says.

▶ Edit accessories. For a clean, spare look, each bedside table holds an oversize lamp, *above right.* "We like big things that make a statement instead of a lot of little things," Vicki says.

BIG ACCESSORIES

LEATHER AND WOOD

BIG ACCESSORIES

WINE

LEATHER AND WOOD

▶**SIMPLE WINDOW TREATMENTS.**
Shutters work really well for their uncluttered look. "When the shutters are wide open you can see to the front yard. When closed, it's really private," Vicki says. They use silhouette blinds in the bedrooms.

▶**ARTWORK.** "We bring in color with art," Kirk says. He painted the Statue of Liberty that hangs above the stairway (see page 157) after the first trip he and Vicki took together to New York City. They also hang the work of other artists, preferring a look that's relaxed,

natural, or somewhat tongue-in-cheek. "The pieces always express a sense of humor," she says.

▶**BASIC OR NO FRAMES.** Kirk and Vicki often hang an unframed painted canvas on the wall. Sometimes paint drips show on the canvas sides. That's okay with this couple. They may use a wood or metal frame around other pieces of art.

▶**BIG ACCESSORIES.** Fewer and bigger pieces are a better choice for this design

duo. Oversize ceramic containers painted in stripes and dots stand taller than the living room sofa. A huge fishbowl (see page 151) sits on the kitchen counter. With a mix of plants, snails, and fish, it's low maintenance and dramatic.

▶**WINE.** Kirk built a wine closet just off the family room using wine crates. A French door keeps his display within easy view.

▶**STOOLS AND SMALL TABLES.** Flexible and movable, these small pieces of furniture

STOOLS

appear throughout Kirk and Vicki's home. Some are used as occasional tables; others end up in the shower.

▶LETTERS. Kirk always searches flea markets and junk shops for large letters from vintage signs. He likes the graphic impact of placing just one oversize letter on a wall.

▶LEATHER AND WOOD. Clean-lined furniture that mixes leather with wood offer the perfect expression of their look.

BUSINESS BASICS Kirk Schlupp and Vicki Semke opened their first Mig and Tig home furnishings store partly to sell their own designs, partly to carry the work of other vendors. "It finally got to the point where we had to decide what to be—wholesalers, designers, or retailers," Vicki says. They chose retail and plunged headfirst into creating a recognizable look for the Chicago market.

Last year they tweaked their look once again, focusing more on upholstery and dining room furniture. The look is what Kirk and Vicki call "organic modern."

MIG AND TIG (CHICAGO)
ADDRESS 549 N. Wells Street
PHONE 312/644-8277

MIG AND TIG
(WINNETKA, ILLINOIS)
ADDRESS 910 N. Green Bay Road
PHONE 847/784-9212
WEBSITE www.migandtig.com

Caroline Verschoor and Jon–Paul Saunier

shopkeepers

Ekster

vintage and new furniture, home accessories, and jewelry

LEESBURG, VIRGINIA

sentimental shopkeepers

Above: Caroline Verschoor and Jon-Paul Saunier enclosed the front porch to create more living space. The stone walls and floor provide a textured backdrop for their mix of rustic farm furniture and dressy French pieces. They shortened the table legs to create the coffee table.

Both modern and classic upholstered frames get the same treatment: covers of creamy unbleached linen.
Opposite: Caroline loves to keep the patina of old chairs but freshen them with new upholstery. The console table is a new copy of a vintage piece.

vintage

or new, some pieces in Caroline Verschoor and Jon-Paul Saunier's home just might be for sale if you ask. Other pieces wouldn't be for sale at any price. The reason, of course, is sentiment. As shopkeepers they sell boatloads of furniture and accessories to make a living. But some of the pieces in their home hold memories that make them so dear that these shopkeepers hold on tight. Caroline and Jon-Paul understand how material objects can produce strong emotions and tug at the heart.

They know, too, that it's possible to create the perfect home without living in the perfect house. They bought their 1,900-square-foot stone cottage for its location, the beautiful land around it, and a good school district. The house, says Caroline, "was a little dumpy." After five years of work, they managed to add a new roof and central heat and air, refinish floors, remove ceilings to reveal beams, take down old walls to open up rooms, replace all the windows, enclose the front porch, and remodel the kitchen and bathroom. And they've filled the house with memories.

Although Caroline still longs for high ceilings and big windows, she applied her design talents to the stone cottage with its small windows and dark interiors. The lesson? Adapt the style you like to the space you're in. Although Caroline loves color, white was the perfect choice to make the ceilings, which are less than 8 feet, seem higher and the rooms seem lighter. The floors, too, lightened up after sanding and bleaching. "I cannot emphasize enough that each house has its own unique demands," she says.

To make the little house work for their young family, they added storage in new built-ins and vintage cupboards. They hung mirrors to reflect the light, installed low-voltage contemporary lights to supplement sunlight, and simplified everything from window coverings to upholstery. They bought a scrubbed-top table that can stand up to daily wear, turned a coffee-table-size trunk into toy storage, and covered sofas with washable slipcovers.

Although they sold just about everything they owned when they moved from their contemporary 3,000-square-foot loft in Washington, D.C., to this cottage in rural Virginia, they held onto their art collection. "I think art, when it speaks to you, is priceless," Caroline says. Just like the cherished mirror her son gave her or the sampler stitched by a friend in her native Holland.

Caroline imported the romantic bed canopy from Holland. It's the perfect solution for their space-starved bedroom. She also tea-stained toile, then used it to slipcover a modern leather chair that moved with them from their loft.

Opposite left: To open up their kitchen, they removed the ceiling to expose beams, discarded upper cabinets, and painted everything white. Bare windows let the light in.

Opposite right: Storage is a challenge in a small house so Caroline and Jon-Paul built a wall of bookcases in their dining room. The table and chairs are new pieces that look old. Modern lighting adds a surprising touch.

Caroline kept the living room simple
with white walls and bleached floors.
The Roman shades were made from
Dutch linen. The antique pier mirror
and French terra-cotta statue add
elegance. It's a hardworking space,
too, with toys stored in the oversize
wicker trunk and slipcovered sofas that
stand up to two busy preschoolers.

**JON-PAUL SAUNIER AND
CAROLINE VERSCHOOR**

Vintage and modern pieces from Europe in a simple stone cottage

▶ Start with natural tones. Caroline suggests picking paint colors—always drawn from nature—based on your house. "The house we live in is so small and has very little natural light, so I used creamy paints to open up the space," Caroline says. "I would not always recommend white paint." Earthy tones, pretty slate blues, grays, sage greens, and buttery yellows all offer colors from nature. Consider, too, the colors of weathered woods, seashells, a spring fern, and pretty hydrangeas. "These are all inspirational colors to me."

▶ Lighten up the floors. If your floors are dark, Caroline recommends stripping and bleaching to get them as light as possible. If you don't have wood floors, light ceramic tile will do. Stay away from polyurethane finishes because they look too artificial. Then use sisal or sea-grass rugs.

▶ Keep window treatments minimal. If you don't need coverings for privacy, leave the windows bare. To keep the sun out, only Roman shades will do, Caroline says.

▶ Group your collections. Caroline gathers her collections on open shelves, in cupboards, and on cabinet tops. "Collections are fine but shouldn't be scattered about," she says.

▶ Use big and small ideas for storage. "I love sorting and storing," Caroline says. "This is a small house and we need all the space we have." New built-in bookcases and vintage cupboards offer lots of space to hold everyday gear. For open shelves Caroline uses metal or wicker baskets. "I'll do anything to hide the mess," she explains. Wall recesses over the bathtub, shelves above the bedroom doorways, and pegs under the windowsills in the children's bedrooms offer snippets of storage.

▶ Combine modern with vintage. In the kitchen Jon-Paul and Caroline paired stainless-steel appliances and stools with open shelves and white-painted cabinets. They added contemporary low-voltage lighting throughout the first floor.

▶ Upholster old sofa and chair frames. "I love old frames and buy them by the boatload, literally," Caroline says. She works with a local upholsterer who covers the frames in everything from bolt-end toiles to painter's dropcloths. Some go to the shop; others go home.

"OBJETS TROUVÉS"

STORAGE

CANDLES

ART

▶**CANDLES.** "I don't care if it's summer," Caroline says. She uses them around the house, set in sand in the bottom of an old chicken feeder, placed in a row on a deep window ledge, or standing alone on a table.

▶**MIRRORS, PREFERABLY OLD.** In a small house, they reflect space and spread sunlight around.

▶ **"OBJETS TROUVÉS."** These are the objects that create an emotional response. For Caroline that includes shells, old pictures, silverplate pieces, and statues.

▶**ART.** "I think my first real salary was spent on a beautiful painting," she says. Buying art or following an artist is really an affair of the heart. "It's like falling in love. If you choose well, there's never a reason to trade it in or up," she says. Caroline doesn't hang a lot on the walls but what goes up is priceless.

▶**STORAGE.** "Extra storage is always welcome, clutter is not," Caroline says. She uses baskets, bowls, hooks, and pegs. Even the coffee table in the living room eliminates clutter. It's filled to the brim with toys.

BUSINESS BASICS Caroline and Jon-Paul didn't set out to be shopkeepers. Caroline just started going to auctions. With a great eye for style, she found it easy to sell the objects she bought. Her business grew, and she started shopping in her native Holland. Before long Jon-Paul left his job in Washington, D.C., and joined Caroline in the business. They continued to sell through Lucketts General Store in Lucketts, Virginia, then opened their own store, called Ekster, in Leesburg, Virginia, *left* and *above right*.

They recently moved their well-edited collection of furniture, accessories, jewelry, and artwork to a larger shop. They import much of the inventory from Europe. "Because we shop the European markets and have many 'pickers' there, we are able to find our customers eclectic pieces that are unique and affordable," she says. "Everything is handpicked by us. Our personal stamp of approval is on it."

EKSTER

ADDRESS 105 S. King Street, Leesburg, VA 20176   **PHONE** 703/771-1784
WEBSITE www.eksterantiques.com   **E-MAIL** ewanthebrave@hotmail.com

photo stylists

On work days photo stylists see the world through the lens of a camera. Sometimes they create room settings or product setups from scratch. Other times they make a wonderful house look even better for the camera. They're always working for a client, creating beautiful photographs for a book, magazine, or catalog. Exposed to a world of style and the best ideas of designers from coast to coast, they know what it takes to make them happy at home. They also know what it takes to make their own homes picture perfect.

"In styling rooms, it's better to have one big thing than a bunch of little things. Big has impact; small makes clutter."

—MARY MULCAHY, LES INDIENNES

"*I've trained my eye to see rooms like a camera sees them. It has changed the way I look at space.*"
—JOETTA MOULDEN, SHELTERSTYLE

"*I like the visual tranquillity of the neutrals. I like color but I want it to stand out when I use it.*"
—LYNN STEELY, LYNN STEELY ANTIQUES AND ART

"*Putting something unexpected in a photograph adds a sense of surprise.*"
—JIMMIE CRAMER, SEVEN GATES FARM

the garden within

Jimmie Cramer

photostylist, style-editor-at-large for Country Home® magazine

Seven Gates Farm

KEEDYSVILLE, MARYLAND

Both rustic and elegant, the garden room offers a resting spot with a view of the gardens. Jimmie Cramer made the "clock" using numbers from an English lawn game and vintage clock hands. He dressed down the French ottoman with rustic linen tacked in place.

Opposite: A pitcher of white alliums brings the garden into the studio. Charcoal walls silhouette vintage white furniture and fabrics.

some designers seek out museums when they feel the need for inspiration; others take shopping trips to foreign cities. Jimmie Cramer turns homeward.

"I go to the garden," he says. You'll find him there with clippers in hand, taming a round ball of boxwood or snipping a spent white bloom, imagining what he can create next.

After all, it's the garden that lives within his soul that serves as his true design compass, leading to a home and yard that blend seamlessly. It's a haven he created with longtime partner Dean Johnson, who died unexpectedly last winter. They dubbed their Maryland home and its surrounding gardens Seven Gates Farm.

Above: "Walls" of clipped boxwood enclose the outdoor dining room. Rocks and moss underfoot create a "rug."
Opposite: Charcoal paint accents the architecture in the dining room. Jimmie removed the ceiling and whitewashed the beams to lighten the space. Grinding stones serve as pedestals on the table.

When Jimmie and Dean moved to the 1800s farmhouse in the mid-1980s, the two-story house and surrounding acre of land were waiting for their touch. They suspected that treasures lay hidden inside the old house, but carpeting, dropped ceilings, drywall, and a kitchen remodeling veiled most of the vintage character. Outside only four large maple trees, one rose bush, and a grape arbor had taken root.

"We were so anxious to start gardening that we moved the herb garden to a spot outside the kitchen door six months before we had the house ready to move into," Jimmie says.

Then they went to work inside, pulling away years of remodeling mistakes and revealing the bones of the old house. "We took it piece by piece, hoping," Jimmie says. They pried away cheap kitchen cabinets and carpeting and found log walls, a walk-in fireplace, and original plank flooring. They tore down ceilings to reveal the timbers that framed the pre-Civil War home. They removed Victorian additions to the front porch and rebuilt it to match the home's original porch using an early photograph for reference.

The style of the house is now primitive and modern. Although the furnishings and collections draw from the past, their use is both fresh and surprising. Contemporary track lighting hangs from rustic beams, new galvanized garden chairs slip under a primitive farm table, and white-slipcovered ladder-back chairs stand in stark relief against charcoal-painted wainscoting.

The revamped spaces house collections—stone and metal urns, rustic linen and homespun, handblown glass, white-painted furniture, garden ornaments, galvanized buckets, and ironstone.

Castoffs became useful again. They made sconces from old shovels, adapted grindstones as table pedestals, and turned metal trash cans and buckets into storage containers.

"Someone told me that everything is where it should be in my house," Jimmie says. "It's not too sparse, and it's not too cluttered."

As the home took shape, so did the gardens. Jimmie and Dean didn't set out to create rooms, but as they planted shrubs and small trees and built fences and gates, they created enclosed spaces they really liked. They planted these rooms with unusual specimens, some valued for their foliage, some for their flowers.

Now as you circle the yard, you'll walk past the white garden with its allium globes, the vegetable garden and greenhouse, the weather vane garden just beyond the garden house, and the sitting garden underplanted with creeping thyme. Every spot has a place to sit, either a galvanized bench or a garden table and chairs. "It's like having dining and living rooms inside and out," Jimmie says.

Now almost 20 years later, the house and garden still serve as an ever-changing canvas for Jimmie's creativity. But no matter what new ideas spring from his walks, they always reflect the soul of a gardener.

Right: *Stainless-steel benches add a modern touch to the garden sitting area. A rock path planted with creeping thyme stretches between the benches.*
Opposite: *Pieces from the garden mix with reproduction chairs and antiques in the living room. Jimmie likes to cut grasses or blooms and place them in blown-glass vases. He pairs modern track lighting with candle fixtures so he can create just the mood he wants.*

CUSTOM HATCHING
2¢ an egg or 4¢ a Chix
Turkeys 3¢ an egg or 5¢ a Chix
Ducks 3¢ an egg or 5¢ a Duckling
ALLEN KELLER

*Jimmie reversed the downstairs color
scheme in the upstairs studio, painting
the walls charcoal and the trim white.
He designed the rustic worktable using
galvanized pipe and industrial casters.
New metal boxes provide storage on
a vintage shelf.*

A collection of favorite metal pieces creates a picture-perfect vignette on the front porch. "The plant stand is so sculptural, it didn't need any plants," Jimmie says.

Above: Jimmie framed pages from an old herbarium to create a wall of art for his bedroom. Warm brown covers the walls.
Above right: On the kitchen mantel, watering-can nozzles fill a berry-picking basket repaired with canvas. The transferware cup features a gardener.

Center right: A leather club chair and daybed in the barn offer a comfy spot to rest from gardening. The long table is a potting bench.
Below right: Grasses mix with succulents in a garden urn. Jimmie likes to dry grasses and use them inside.

JIMMIE CRAMER

Muted colors,
modern metals, and
rustic collections in
an 1800s house

IN THE HOUSE

▶ Collect American white-painted furniture.
Combine all shades of old white paint.
Old paint looks milky with some crazing.

▶ Use muted colors. "It's all about creating
a background for white-painted furniture,"
Jimmie says. Browns, grays, creams, and
white make up the palette, *opposite*. Use
paint with minimal gloss.

▶ Bring the garden in. He cuts alliums in
spring, hosta leaves in summer, cardoon
leaves and grasses in the fall, and dried
berries in winter. A single leaf or bloom is
just right. Garden elements, such as urns,
flower frogs, and tools, add to the look.

▶ Place objects perfectly. "Sometimes a
space calls for one simple item because it
makes more of a statement," he says. He
likes to create unusual pairings such as a
chrome television with handhewn log walls or
ironstone with well-used brushes, *above center*.

▶ Install track lighting. Track lights offer
flexibility and hide behind ceiling beams.
He uses lamps only in the bedrooms.

▶ Leave floors bare. "I used to put rugs
down for fall and winter, but it closes in
a room and makes islands," he says.

IN THE GARDEN

▶ Pick a simple color scheme. Jimmie plants
flowers with blooms of white or an
almost black shade of maroon or purple.
The blooms look good inside as well.

▶ Create garden rooms. Jimmie uses plants
as architecture, letting their shapes make
"walls" and "ceilings." Slices of rock
create "floors." Garden chairs and tables
furnish the rooms, *above right*.

▶ Create a focal point in every garden. Plant
a garden along a fence with a trellised
gate or place an urn as the view from a
garden bench.

▶ Layer textures. For contrast he pairs leafy
ferns with tight boxwood leaves and sprays
of grasses with lavender spikes.

▶ Bring the house to the garden. In the
barn leather furniture provides seating.
The garden room holds garden books.
Galvanized-metal tables outside mirror
the kitchen's galvanized countertop.

HOMESPUN

OLD WHITE PAINT

▶**IRONSTONE.** Jimmie collects what he calls "dirty ironstone," pieces with a white surface turned brown from age and use. He especially loves pieces with cracks. His collection includes mostly compotes, but he also has platters, punch bowls, mixing bowls, pitchers, and plates.

▶**CUT FLOWERS.** "No bought flowers," Jimmie says. He picks everything in his garden, from hosta leaves to branches with berries. In the late fall and winter, he brings in dried branches. He may cluster a bunch of leaves in a container or place a single bloom in a handblown glass vase.

▶**POTTED PLANTS.** The easiest plants to keep alive inside include ficus trees, fig trees, and succulents. Potted plants fill the garden, too, allowing Jimmie to decorate an outdoor room or to create a sense of enclosure.

▶**BLOWN GLASS.** It doesn't matter to Jimmie if it's old glass or new. It's all about shape. He has everything from big leech bowls to small cruets. "You have to look for stuff that's a little unusual instead of the ordinary," Jimmie says about collecting in general. "You have to be a shopper and keep your eyes open for what's different."

▶**URNS.** Spread throughout the garden and the house, urns provide containers for plants and drama underneath track lighting. Jimmie collects American and European urns and owns metal, stone, and concrete pieces.

▶**GALVANIZED METAL.** "Galvanized objects and surfaces have a modern look when paired with primitive pieces," Jimmie says. The metal appears as kitchen chairs, countertops, table and bench tops in the

garden, buckets and bins for plants, and even as storage containers in the office.

▶**WHITE AND CREAM POTTERY.** Jimmie collects McCoy pots and Haeger vases and uses them inside and out. He loves the Haeger pieces for their clean, modern shapes.

▶**HOMESPUN.** Just as with ironstone, Jimmie searches for off-white fabrics that have been aged by time. He uses the linen and homespun as slipcovers for his dining chairs, to cover furniture in his garden house, or as pillows and wall hangings. "I like the earthy texture of it and the muted colors," he says.

▶**CONCRETE AND STONE.** "These pieces really reflect my love of texture and shape," Jimmie says. He collects urns and garden statuary, displays grinding stones in both the

RNS

IRONSTONE

CUT FLOWERS

HOMESPUN

GARDEN ELEMENTS

garden and the dining room, and uses stone footwarmers for hot pans in the kitchen.

►GARDEN ELEMENTS. Jimmie searches for things that remind him of the garden. That's why you'll find an extensive collection of early garden photography, seed packets and labeled seed jars, herbariums, garden books, sprinkler heads, trowels and rakes, and terrariums. He uses the pieces both inside and out.

►OLD WHITE PAINT. Jimmie is drawn to interesting shapes, but they all look better to him if the surface is a milky shade of white. The pieces might be architectural elements, vintage furniture, or even small objects. Take care when you buy white-painted pieces. Old paint should be worn from use. Avoid pieces with fake wear created with sandpaper.

BUSINESS BASICS As a style-editor-at-large for *Country Home*® magazine, Jimmie Cramer creates house and garden projects for photography. His work appears in these books: *Quick Country Decorating* (Meredith Books, 2000); *Windowboxes Indoors and Out* (Artisan, 1999), and *Seasons at Seven Gates Farm* (Hearst, 1996).

Jimmie also sells antiques through a local shop, Beaver Creek Antiques Market in Maryland. His inventory includes ironstone and pantry boxes.

ADDRESS Beaver Creek Antiques Market
20202 National Pike
Hagerstown, Maryland 21740
PHONE 301/739-8075
WEBSITE www.beavercreekantiques.com

Joetta Moulden
photo stylist and interior designer

ShelterStyle

HOUSTON, TEXAS

quick-change artistry

Above: *Joetta Moulden gave her living room a new look by editing and rearranging what she had and adding color. Terra-cotta color paint adds a fresh look to the backs of the bookcases and makes her collections stand out.*
Opposite: *Favorite pieces cluster on a tabletop. Joetta likes to combine objects that reflect the color palette of the room.*

change comes easily to Joetta Moulden. It's not

surprising. She grew up in a creative home and moved with her parents to a new Frank Lloyd Wright–inspired house every 4 to 5 years. Through all the moves just one interior designer helped her parents incorporate the same furnishings from house to house. "In each house the furnishings looked completely different," Joetta says.

It's little wonder Joetta's work life reflects the lessons she learned at home. On some days she styles houses for photo shoots for interior design publications. On other days she visits clients' homes as part of her business called ShelterStyle. In this role she works with clients, showing them how to redecorate their homes with a few inexpensive changes, using much of the furniture and accessories they already own. "I never tire of seeing how people take the same four walls and a roof and make it their own world."

But Joetta's rearranging doesn't stop with her list of clients. "To this day I love change," she says. "I can't move that often, but I can and do change my interiors often." The changes can be small or big—painting the back of her living room bookshelves, moving furniture, ordering a new focal-point rug, organizing books and treasures on tabletops and cabinets, or arranging fresh flowers until they're perfect.

"I've trained my eye to see rooms like a camera sees them," she says. "It has changed the way I look at space." Now she notices subtle details that throw a room off balance—one white picture mat in a sea of cream mats on a wall, an unbalanced color that makes a room seem lopsided, or a piece of art that's hung too high above a sofa or a headboard. The lens of a camera provides such a good view of interior design that she shares this tip with clients: When you think you have everything just right in a room, take some snapshots. Any problems will jump out of the photographs.

"I'm just lucky my hobby is my profession," she says. "Very few people get to do what they really want to do."

JOETTA MOULDEN

Collected objects and punches of color in a basic 1950s ranch

▶ Start with a neutral backdrop. "If you like change, the best thing is a neutral backdrop," Joetta says. She used a soft mushroom color for the walls, then painted the bookshelf backs, *opposite*. In one day her living room had a brand new colorful focus for only $13 in materials.

▶ Select neutral fabrics. They offer a basic backdrop. Replace pillows or re-cover the chair seats, *above right,* for a change that's more economical than updating upholstery. "You're looking at a thousand dollars in

upholstery and fabric," Joetta says. "I can do my changes for pennies."

▶ Top hardwood floors with rugs. For her own living room, Joetta asked artist Lisa Frisco to paint a sisal rug, *above center*. Joetta also suggests cutting berber carpeting to rug size and binding the edges.

▶ Contrast textures for interest. She loves to play cotton velvet against silk, add fringe to linen, or set silver on rough wood. It's a technique that helps tone down formal pieces, such as the inherited crystal decanters, which sit in an antique basket with wicker-wrapped bottles.

▶ Fill your home with art. "I cannot imagine being happy without being surrounded by art," she says. Hang art so it relates to the table or sofa beneath it, or hang it in unexpected places such as on the frame of a bookcase or in a window.

▶ Use curtain panels. They soften a wall's hard edges, finish a room, and visually raise low ceilings. Pair them with blinds, shades, or shutters for privacy.

▶ Add your own touches. Joetta likes to comb-paint furniture and frames or make her own mats. "The bonus is that you will not walk into your neighbor's house and see the same frame," she says.

▶ Have some fun. Joetta couldn't afford to create a wall of Mexican masks because each mask cost $350. Instead she bought carved coconut heads at a seashell store. "They're all hysterically funny," she says. "I hung them seriously, but they aren't."

▶ Use antique accessories. "What keeps a room from looking like a gift shop is the weathered softness that an antique engraving, frame, box, or platter brings to a space," she explains.

FAUX VINTAGE PRINTS

BASKETS

BASKETS

▶WHITE IRONSTONE. "I just like the cleanliness and simplicity of it," she says. She mixes new and old pieces and collects them in a range from cream to pure white.

▶ANTIQUE WOODEN TROUGHS. "I like the ones that have mends," she says. She collects vintage pieces and uses them to hold rocks collected on Cape Cod or rose petals saved from photo shoots.

▶BASKETS. Joetta uses both vintage and new baskets. "They're wonderful to corral clutter," she says. She keeps them around the house, filling them with everything from magazines to wicker-wrapped bottles. They provide pretty and portable storage.

▶COLLECTIONS. She loves to collect 18th- and 19th-century Santos, platters, and books. "I like to group things together," she says. "That's one way to intensify the impact of a collection." But Joetta doesn't buy only vintage objects with good pedigrees. "If you mix really good reproductions with the real thing, it elevates the reproductions."

▶FOUND OBJECTS. Joetta incorporates stones, shells, and coral along with seedpods and wasps' nests. The shells hold special memories because she dove for them. "The most personal homes are a reflection of the books you like to read, the things you collect, and the found objects you bring back from trips," she says. Joetta tucks these treasures in baskets or on bookshelves.

▶COFFEE TABLE BOOKS. She loves the way they look stacked on a table, bookshelf, ottoman, or even a chair seat.

▶LARGE-SCALE ACCESSORIES. "I'd rather have one huge whopper vase on a tabletop than a dozen little boxes that may cost three times the cost of the vase," she says.

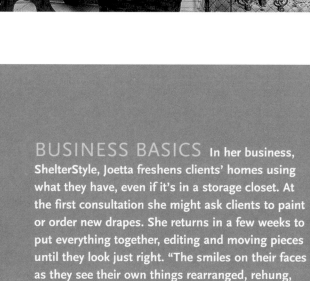

PICTURE FRAMES

▶PICTURE FRAMES. If you go to flea markets, there are lots of empty picture frames. "If you love the frame, you can always cut it down." Old frames can make even photocopies look wonderful. New frames also look good if you personalize them with comb-painting or new mats.

▶FAUX VINTAGE PRINTS. If you buy an old book filled with illustrations, try this trick. Scan the image, then print it on rag paper. "It will look like an antique print," she says.

▶KENNETH TURNER CANDLES. Fragrance can be a great finishing touch.

BUSINESS BASICS In her business, ShelterStyle, Joetta freshens clients' homes using what they have, even if it's in a storage closet. At the first consultation she might ask clients to paint or order new drapes. She returns in a few weeks to put everything together, editing and moving pieces until they look just right. "The smiles on their faces as they see their own things rearranged, rehung, and brought out of closets is pure joy for me."

SHELTERSTYLE

ADDRESS 9337-B Katy Freeway, #176
Houston, Texas 77024

PHONE 713/461-2063

WEBSITE www.shelterstyle.com

E-MAIL joetta@shelterstyle.com

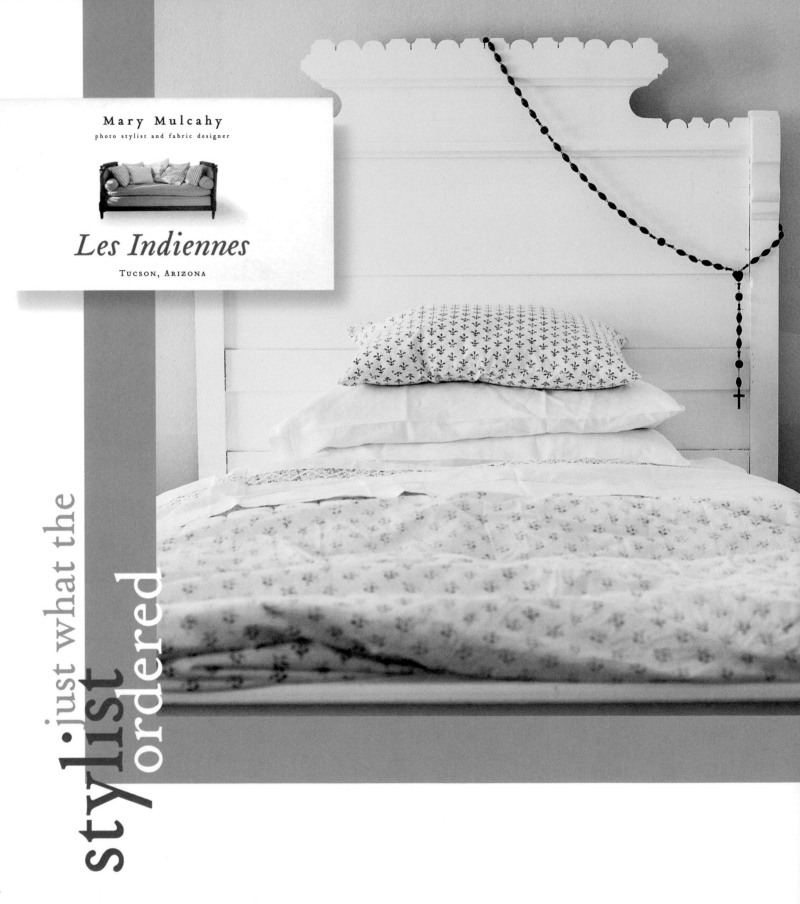

Mary Mulcahy

photo stylist and fabric designer

Les Indiennes

Tucson, Arizona

just what the

stylist

styl·ist ordered

Mary Mulcahy gave her living room a relaxed look by replacing a pink marble fireplace surround with blue and white tile. White slipcovers and walls let her change the look with ease.

Opposite: A Victorian headboard painted white looks refreshing in the master bedroom. The patterned pillowcase and duvet cover showcase the patterns Mary adapted from traditional Indian block-print fabrics.

Left: A narrow console table in the
entryway holds a composition of Mary's
favorite things: her own fabric in blue,
a black-and-white photograph, red
lampshades, and spheres.
Above: To create simplicity at home,
Mary uses color sparingly and reduces
accessories to a chosen few. The rosary
is a favorite keepsake from Lourdes.
Opposite: Mary likes to make daybeds
from twin-bed headboards. "Just put the
two headboards together and throw on
a bunch of feather pillows," Mary says.

making the bed can seem like such a common

everyday task. But when you earn your living styling rooms for
photography, how you dress the bed can be far from routine. Just
ask photo stylist Mary Mulcahy. For more than 20 years she has
regularly styled the stuff of ordinary life for magazines and
catalogs, making it look good enough to buy—or imitate.

She devotes the same attention to detail at home, transforming a
previously formal circa-1929 Spanish Colonial house into a home
she describes as family-friendly and down-to-earth.

To simplify her home, Mary removed marble tiles and grand
chandeliers, replacing them with pieces more suitable to the look
of a Provençal farmhouse. She painted the walls in an understated
palette of warm white. Window treatments, such as shutters and
fabric panels, offer protection from the sun but fade into the
background. Slipcovers dress down formal upholstered frames, and
a few perfectly placed accessories create focal points. The neutral
backdrop of walls and floors allows her to change the pillows,
accessories, and furniture arrangements on a whim.

Some of the tricks she uses in photo styling and in her own home offer inspiration. To add a bit of color to a room, she paints only the bottom half of walls in just a few areas or brings in color with pillows or collections. To create a sense of surprise, she might use a tablecloth as a throw over an armchair or top slender lamp bases with bright red shades.

Her look, though, remains simple and edited. "When I'm styling rooms, I've learned that it's better to have one big object on a mantel or tabletop than a bunch of little things," she says.

It's the same less-is-more strategy she incorporated into the design of a line of fabrics for her new company, Les Indiennes. Based on traditional Indian block-print designs, these hand-printed fabrics capture Mary's style perfectly. They combine a minimal color scheme (white plus one color) with basic designs pulled from traditional allover patterns. Printed on soft, washed cotton, they offer the casual look and easy care that's perfect for today's relaxed living. It's just what the stylist ordered.

Above right: *Vintage pieces get a new look thanks to a loose-fitting slipcover or fresh paint. Mary finds new pieces, such as the lamps, on the Internet.*

Above left: *A mixture of white tableware in a white cupboard gives Mary the serene interiors she prefers. She suggests that you paint every wall white when you first move into a new home, then gradually add color.*

Opposite: *A silhouette brings drama to the breakfast room. Mary added chair pads for comfort and painted the cabinet. "If a piece is really nice, I won't paint it," she says.*

A daybed in her home office shows how Mary uses white plus one color to create her look. The poster reminds Mary of her days as a fashion photo stylist. **Opposite:** A wall of bookshelves opposite the daybed holds Mary's collection of decorating books. She snuggled her grandfather's desk into the alcove and added crystal sconces for a surprising touch.

MARY MULCAHY

Dressed-down furniture and unfussy fabrics in a picture-perfect home

▶ Use a few colors. Mary uses an off-white paint throughout her home. If she adds color, it's one color plus white. Her favorites? Gray blues and pink reds used sparingly. "Sometimes I feel a little color on a wall goes a long way, so I paint a half-wall," she says. She also likes to add color to the floor, *opposite*.

▶ Stitch slipcovers. Mary slipcovers headboards, sofas, and chairs, adding dressmaker details such as pleats, gathers, or ties, *above right*. "I don't want them

too fussy," she says. "Sometimes it's fun to put one little tuck in the corner of a chair to liven it up."

▶ Layer colorful pillows and throws. They let her change the look seasonally and add a punch of color where she wants it. She uses her own fabric line for pillows and throws in the warm months, then switches to faux fur pillows in winter.

▶ Opt for scale. "I love to use twenty-six-inch European-style pillows on a big sofa. They are the best to curl up on and sleep," she says. She also incorporates oversize paintings, tall lamps, and a few large pieces of furniture. "Big is better," she says. "Small makes clutter."

▶ Relax the look. Although Mary loves crystal chandeliers, she hangs them in ways that are neither formal nor fussy. "I love to mix crystal with rustic," she says. She also

uses sea-grass mats for hardwood floors, tablecloths on formal tables, and utility fabrics, such as cotton duck, for slipcovers.

▶ Hang curtains in doorways. Mary softens doorways with fabric drapes. "They're romantic," she says.

▶ Simplify window treatments. Shutters offer a classic look. Mary also ties simple curtains on iron rods. "Always hang the curtain higher than the window to make the window seem taller," she says.

▶ Move your furniture. She puts felt pads on furniture legs so it's easy to slide the pieces on hardwood floors.

▶ Edit your collections. Mary loves objects with great shapes and colors but uses them sparingly at home, *above center*. "I see so much and work with so much that I like it really simple at home," she says.

WHITE SHEETS

NEW AND VINTAGE LINENS

▶**WHITE SHEETS.** There just is no substitute for crisp white cotton sheets when it comes to dressing a bed. "I usually try to find the old ones," she says. "They have the crisp feel I love."

▶**WHITE TABLEWARE.** It doesn't matter if the dishes are new or old. "I like white dishes because food looks best on them," she says.

▶**SPHERES.** Mary collects spheres in all sizes and then corrals them in containers. The coffee table in her living room showcases a collection of sea-grass balls in a Mexican bowl; a wood tray in the entry holds blue and white spheres.

▶**PERFUME BOTTLES.** A platter serves as the perfect perch for Mary's collection of perfume bottles. "I just love the shapes of the bottles," she says.

▶**BOOKS.** Mary stores her huge collection of decorating books in bookcases throughout the house, but keeps many of them in her home office. She also uses books as pedestals for other accessories.

▶**CHAIRS.** "I really love different styles of chairs," she says. She slipcovers or upholsters them or uses them "as is" throughout her house, including in the bathrooms. Her best buy was an Eames chair she bought at Goodwill for $9.99.

▶**BEDS.** Mary often switches one headboard for another. The headboard might get a coat of paint or a slipcover before it returns to the house. Where does she store the extras? "I have a really large garage," she admits. She also likes to create a daybed by sandwiching a twin mattress between a set of twin headboards.

▶**LES INDIENNES.** Mary loves to use pieces from her line of fabrics, bedding, and papers. They perfectly fit her decorating tip: use just one color with white.

▶**SCREENS.** Screens are great in a bathroom as a half-wall around a toilet, to divide a large room into more intimate

PERFUME BOTTLES

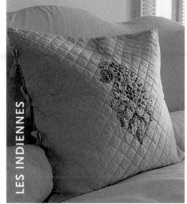

LES INDIENNES

CHAIRS

SCREENS

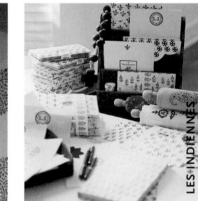

LES INDIENNES

seating areas, or to create a movable
window treatment. Mary likes to refresh
screens with fabric.

▶NEW AND VINTAGE LINENS. Mary's
collection includes old towels and good
reproductions. She places them on top of
dressers, in serving baskets, and on tables.
"I use them all the time for photo styling,"
she says.

▶OLD MEDICAL LIGHTING. Industrial-
looking lamps in stainless steel or other
metals add an unexpected modern touch to
the interiors. Mary collects lamps once used
in doctors' offices and photography studios,
pairing them with soft furniture.

BUSINESS BASICS

It was love at first
sight when Mary found two bolts of an Indian block-
print fabric during a trip to Toronto a few years
back. She couldn't find the fabric anywhere so she
put an ad on Indian Mart on the Internet. The reply
started her new business. Mary then spent months
simplifying traditional block prints into the hand-
washed and hand-printed cotton fabrics she now sells
through her web site, www.lesindiennes.com. The
fabrics, as well as a new line of stationery, feature
timeless block prints in three color combinations:
indigo and white, red and white, and gold and white.
"They all go together," she says. "The patterns and
colors are very calming and soothing." Mary also
imports duvet covers, throws, quilts, and pillows
made from the fabrics.

LES INDIENNES
PHONE 520/326-4172
FAX 520/881-5142
WEBSITE www.lesindiennes.com

paradise found

Lynn Steely

photo stylist and interiors editor

Lynn Steely
Antiques and Art

KANSAS CITY, MISSOURI

Lynn Steely affectionately calls the table in her living room a "cowboy coffee table because it's great for putting your feet up," she says. French club chairs add comfortable and stylish seating.
Opposite: Lynn loves to fill her favorite vase with roses in just one color.

rocks

rocks discarded behind her friend's shop. An Empire sofa from a garage sale. A half-round piece of wood left along the road. These objects stop Lynn Steely in her tracks. After all beauty, for Lynn, exists in almost any discarded object. Each treasure offers a little bit of heaven for this magazine editor, interior design writer, antiques dealer, and jewelry designer.

See 'em, love 'em, use 'em. That's Lynn's decorating philosophy. "I'm an as-I-find-it kind of gal. I'm not a project person. I may see them for a different use but not in a different form. I'm not a painter, scraper, or wallpaper hanger," she says.

Making good use of what you have or what you find makes perfect design sense to Lynn. "Sometimes limiting your parameters and narrowing your search or using what you have can inspire greater creativity than the endless search with the endless budget for the perfect object," she says.

She puts that philosophy to work at home by creating a serene backdrop using muted neutrals. She brings in color and trendy items with easily replaced objects, such as flowers, textiles, lamps, and accessories. "If beaded pillows are in, get those," she says, but leave the hot pink sofa at the store. The muted neutrals allow her to incorporate upholstered pieces, such as the dining room chairs, without repainting or reupholstering the chairs.

But don't think Lynn stops looking when she fills up her apartment. "I'm compelled to change out my environment," she admits. She recycles objects through her antiques business or by giving to friends. Although Lynn loves great style, she's not attached to specific objects. If she gets rid of one piece, she'll find another equally fun piece to replace it.

"Live with style, enjoy what you find, and don't obsess about what you have or don't have," Lynn says.

Right: Lynn loves to use garden pieces inside. Branches from the neighborhood become Christmas trees during the holiday. A stack of rocks supports the bare branches. "I use them [rocks] inside because I like the contrast," she says.
Opposite: Books stored in the corner cupboards hint at the second use for the dining room. Chairs from the 1930s, covered in an allover print, offer comfortable seating.

LYNN STEELY

Found objects
and a neutral
palette in a vintage
apartment

► Consider how your space should work. "A lot of us back into our decorating and then make the room work around what we put in it," Lynn says. For her it's as easy as making sure the bedside stand has a drawer for scissors because she clips coupons in bed, *above center*.

► Pick a consistent color palette. The core palette includes whites, off-whites, and browns. She brings in seasonal accents: orange in spring and summer, scarlet red in fall and through the holidays, and muted blue in the winter. The moss-green hue stays all year. "I like to change the accent colors seasonally, but I like the visual tranquillity of neutrals," she says.

► Mix country and antique Asian furnishings. Lynn loves the way rough country pieces look with more formal-lined Asian pieces. Clean lines and honest finishes help pieces harmonize. To create friction she adds clear glass and metal pieces.

► Use a little black and white in every room. The sharpness of this color combination in photography and other objects brings any room up to date. "Plus it helps me integrate electronic equipment, which is contemporary and often black and white," she says.

► Keep it spare. "My look is to create a room that's sparse with nothing superfluous except the occasional piece of art, a natural item, or a whimsical vignette," she says. "And I consider art and nature to be essentials," *above right*.

► Keep extras handy but out of sight. "I actually have a prop closet full of textiles, candles and holders, vases, and odds and ends," Lynn says. "It really is my only 'excess,' and I edit it constantly." When company is coming, she brings out more than she typically displays every day.

► Purchase excellent lighting. Lynn loves pairs of lamps. "I'm sort of a symmetrical person," she admits. An inexpensive lamp, pointed in the right direction, can make great accent or task lighting, *opposite*.

► Develop a few decorating trademarks. Lynn, for example, wraps sheets, towels, and blankets with vintage leather belts. She always displays twigs and shells around her apartment.

WHITE OR SCARLET TOWELS

GARDEN OBJECTS

ARTWORK

FLOWERS AND PLANTS

▶VINTAGE METAL FLOOR LAMPS. "I like the funky medical-dental ones and use them just the way I find them," she says.

▶ARTWORK. Lynn's collection includes photography, paintings, and assemblages. Many of the pieces are from friends; some are her own work.

▶FLOWERS AND PLANTS. "I'm a big rose and herb person," she says. She keeps herbs in the bay window in her studio. For parties Lynn fills a favorite glass vase with one color of roses.

▶GARDEN OBJECTS. Statuary and iron urns come inside because Lynn likes the contrast and the feeling of sculpture they offer an interior. "They look good mixed with browns and leathers," she says.

▶LUGGAGE OF ALL SORTS. Stacks of luggage serve as tables, or a single suitcase might rest on an iron stand that raises it to table height. They all provide storage.

▶NATURAL ITEMS. Lynn loves to fill an urn with coral, stack stones in a birdbath, or place shells on a tabletop. "I like to do groupings," she says. She also uses a section of tree trunk as an end table and gathers branches to display in stone or metal urns. At holiday time the branches become Christmas trees.

▶OLD DRESSMAKERS' FORMS. Lynn displays them as sculpture.

▶EXOTIC TEXTILES AND RUGS. Lynn uses them as throws or wall hangings, preferring sisal rugs on her floors.

▶CLEAR GLASS ACCESSORIES. Domes, cylinders, and pieces of flat glass offer variety. "When you decorate with country furniture and rough textures, glass is a nice complement," Lynn says. "It adds a little glitz and shine." She also makes her own line of lamps using vintage glass pieces.

▶BOOKS. She keeps her collection of books in the corner cupboards in her dining room rather than displaying tableware.

▶WHITE OR SCARLET TOWELS. She changes color by seasons.

▶EVERYDAY ARTIFACTS. Lynn gathers bits and pieces such as handwritten letters and a child's art project. "Then I'll do little vignettes that inspire me, especially around the holidays," she says.

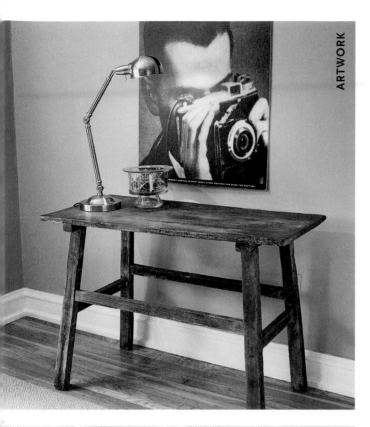

ARTWORK

FLOWERS AND PLANTS

BUSINESS BASICS Lynn Steely has worked at several jobs—photo stylist, interiors editor and writer, jewelry designer, antiques dealer, art dealer, and pillow and evening bag designer. She has her own line of lamps made from vintage pieces. The underlying connection is style.

Her design philosophy crosses from interiors to fashion. She believes in creating a neutral background (a basic black dress or a tan room) then adding color with accessories (great jewelry or a fabulous pillow).

She has been the editor of *Kansas City Home Design* and the primary stylist for Hallmark Flowers. She is an antiques dealer selling at Mission Road Antique Mall in Prairie Village, Kansas, and an artist showing her artwork and jewelry at Curious Sofa in Kansas City.

LYNN STEELY ANTIQUES AND ART

ADDRESS P.O. Box 10164
Kansas City, Missouri 64171

PHONE 816/522-1988

WEBSITE www.lynnsteely.com

SHOPS, WEBSITES, AND SOURCES
Following are some of the favorite shopping spots and product resources of the pros in this book. Some love to shop and offer a long list of stores. Others shop infrequently, viewing it as a chore. Others like to combine trips to Europe with their favorite pastime. Read through the lists for shopping advice and what to look for.

8 FROM BRAD HUNTZINGER:
▶**Aero,** 132 Spring St., New York, NY 10012; 212/966-1500; www.shop@aerostudios.com. Furniture and accessories by Thomas O'Brien.
▶**Amy Perlin Antiques,** 1020 Lexington Ave., 2nd Floor, New York, NY 10021-4223; 212/593-5756. Lots of furniture including traditional French and Italian pieces.
▶**Blackman Cruz,** 800 N. La Cienega Blvd., Los Angeles, CA 90069; 310/657-9228. Brad likes the combination of continental and Asian pieces with a retro, industrial twist to the mix.
▶**Thomas Boog,** Paris. Look for the shop named after the owner/artist at Passage Jouffroy, 10-12 Boulevard Montmartre, 9 Rue de La Grange-Batelière, 9th. Thomas makes incredible lamp bases and more from seashells. "It's expensive, but it's really beautiful," says Brad.
▶**The Gardener,** 1836 4th St., Berkeley, CA 94710; 510/548-4545. Products from furniture to garden books and tabletop. "Great retailer with a great eye."
▶**Takashimaya,** 693 Fifth Ave., New York, NY 10022; 212/350-0100. "It's like a miniature Japanese department store with everything from a garden floral center to bedding to Japanese dishes to jewelry."
▶**Erica Tanov,** 1827 4th St., Berkeley, CA 94710; 510/849-3331. A local clothing designer whose work is carried at Barneys, Erica offers clothing, jewelry, and antiques.
SOURCES IN HOME
Oly furniture and accessories. For a list of retailers, call 510/644-1870 or check www.olystudio.com.

18 FROM ANN SACKS:
SOURCES
▶To find furniture like the midcentury modern pieces in Ann Sacks's home, check out www.knoll.com or www.dwr.com.
▶To find tile, stone, or plumbing fixtures like those used in Ann's home, call 503/281-7751 or check www.annsacks.com.

28 FROM GREGORY EVANS:
▶**Blackman Cruz,** 800 N. La Cienega Blvd., Los Angeles, CA 90069; 310/657-9228. Antiques and unique objects. "I always find something there."
▶**Pat McGann,** 746 N. La Cienega Blvd., Los Angeles, CA 90069; 310/657-8708. Eclectic mix of African artifacts, contemporary art, and antiques. Gregory has shopped there for more than 10 years and always finds a treasure.

38 FROM BROWN/BEDFORD:
▶**Antiques Antiques,** 245 Kansas, San Francisco, CA 94103; 415/252-7600. "A large collection of French armoires and chests," they say.
▶**Art De Asia,** 1235 Sutter St., San Francisco, CA 94109; 415/922-6688. "Large collection of Japanese and Chinese furniture and accessories."
▶**Christiane Millinger Oriental Rugs,** 208 NW 13th Ave., Portland, OR 97210; 503/274-4440. "Great collection of rugs."
▶**Ed Hardy,** 188 Henry Adams St., San Francisco, CA 94103; 415/626-6300. "Wonderful antiques and objects."
▶**French Quarter Linen,** 2325 NW Westover Rd., Portland, OR 97210; 503/241-8436. "Large collection of bedding and bath items."
▶**Gumps,** 135 Post St., San Francisco, CA 94108; 800/766-7628 or www.gumps.com. "We love to shop there for dinnerware and bedding."
▶**J D Madison Rug & Home Co.,** 1307 NW Glisan St., Portland, OR 97209; 503/827-6037. "Carpets, contemporary furniture, and accessories."
▶**MB Accessories,** 200 N. State St., Lake Oswego, OR 97034; 503/635-8188. "Combination of antiques, objects, and lamps."
▶**Takashimaya,** 693 Fifth Ave., New York, NY 10022; 212/350-0100. "Interesting objects and accessories."

50 FROM CARRIE RAPHAEL:
▶**Calico Corners;** www.calicocorners.com. Carrie likes to see what people in the public are looking at and to catch up on Traditions fabrics by Pamela Kline, carried by Calico Corners.
▶**G Street Fabrics,** Potomac Mills, 2700 Potomac Mills Circle #884, Woodbridge, VA 22192; 703/494-5900. See their web site, www.gstreetfabrics.com, for store addresses, phone numbers, and hours for all four locations in the Washington, D.C., area. Carrie loves the store because it's so massive. "The biggest mistake shoppers make is to go to the upholstery area where cotton duck is $25 a yard instead of the dressmakers' fabrics, where it costs $7 a yard," she says. Carrie also buys men's business-shirt fabric to use for Roman shades and slipcovers.
▶**IKEA.** For store locations and catalog, see www.ikea.com. "I know it's inexpensive, but the designs are clever."
▶**www.nordicstyle.com.** "I'm always inspired by something."
▶**Washington Design Center,** 300 D St. SW, Washington, D.C. 20024; 202/646-6118. Retail showrooms on first floor along with special events. Carrie always visits the Country Swedish showroom ("I love their lighting") and the Grange showroom("I go through for inspiration").

62 FROM ELIZABETH GIBSON-WAKEMAN:
Elizabeth shops at antiques auctions in New England and estate sales in Sarasota.
▶**Maine Antiques Festival,** Union, ME. For information on the festival, call Coastal Promotions at 207/563-1013; www.MaineAntiqueFest.com.

Elizabeth attends this show each August. "They have a marvelous collection of Maine antiques dealers."
▶**Marie Selby Botanical Gardens,** 811 S. Palm Ave., Sarasota, FL; 941/366-5731. For more about the gardens, see www.selby.org. Elizabeth checks out their gift shop for orchids and other Florida plants.

72 FROM MARK CLAY:
Mark shops for his job at these antiques events:
▶**Brimfield J&J Promotions,** Brimfield, MA. Call 413/245-3436 or check www.jandj-brimfield.com. The original Brimfield show.
▶**Brimfield May's Antique Market, Inc.,** Brimfield, MA. Call 413/245-9271 or check www.maysbrimfield.com. A field of opportunities for flea market shoppers.
▶**Marburger Farm Antique Show,** Round Top, TX. Call 800/947-5799 or check www.roundtop-marburger.com. Wide range of styles and objects.
▶**Round Top Antiques Fair,** Round Top, TX. Check 281/493-5501 or www.roundtopantiquesfair.com for information about this Emma Lee Turney event. Classic country pieces.

78 FROM VIRGINIA BURNEY:
▶**Badia Design,** 5034 Vineland Ave., North Hollywood, CA 91601; 818/761-2910 or www.badiadesign.com. "Moroccan accessories."
▶**Big People Toys Warehouse,** 2203 1st Ave., Seattle, WA 98121; 206/447-5654. "The owner and his daughter personally brave the interior of China to find unique items."
▶**Cargo,** 1240 NW 14th Ave., Portland, OR 97209; 503/209-8346 or www.cargoinc.com. "Cargo has everything from everywhere."
▶**Casa Reyna,** San Miguel de Allende, Mexico. "Wonderful old primitive items from Mexico."
▶**Chrisman Picture Frames,** 8002 SE 13th Ave., Portland, OR 97202; 503/235-0328. "Fabulous supply of frames and exceptional workmanship."
▶**David Smith & Co.,** 334 Boren Ave. N., Seattle, WA 98109; 206/223-1598 or www.davidsmithco.com. "The best of Indonesia."
▶**Dos Gallos,** 924 N. Formosa Ave., Los Angeles, CA 90046; 323/851-9117 or www.dosgallos.com. "Wonderful furniture from South and Central America."
▶**Euro Pine Imports,** 1030 E. Camelback Rd., Phoenix, AZ 85014; 602/263-0198 or www.europine.com. "Superb restoration of old European pine pieces."
▶**Flowers by Dorcas,** 525 SW Broadway, Portland, OR 97205. "Creative designs and great style."
▶**Holler & Saunder,** Nogales, AZ; 520/287-5153. By appointment only. "They have the most beautiful antiques and collectibles from the Americas and Europe."
▶**Inja,** 700 7th St., #101, San Francisco, CA 94103; 415/255-2204. "Korean pieces with unusual grace."
▶**Naomi's Lampshades,** 15942 SW Boones Ferry Rd., Lake Oswego, OR 97035; 503/636-1884; www.naomislampsandshades.com. "They can make anything into a lamp."
▶**Shogun's Gallery,** 1111 NW 23rd Ave., Portland, OR 97210; 503/224-0328; www.shogunsgallery.com.

"Fine collection of antique Japanese furniture, porcelains, and decorative pieces."
▶**Wiseman & Gale Interiors, Inc.,** 4015 N. Marshall Way, Scottsdale, AZ 85251; 480/945-8447. "Beautiful antique furniture in exquisite condition."

88 FROM STEPHEN KNOLLENBERG:
▶**Amsterdam,** 3483 Blue Star Hwy., Saugatuck, MI 49453; 269/857-3044. "Funky little store in an old barn. They have new and old throughout. You might find a giant white turkey platter that's contemporary but then next to it an old painted chair. The owner has an eye for the electic."
▶**Angus and Company,** 647 Dupont St., Toronto, Ontario M6G1Z4. "Sells old and new. Wonderfully interesting linen napkins, clothes, and beautiful stemware. The place might be piled high with the most exceptional leather suitcases you've ever seen."
▶**Cove Landing,** 995 Lexington Ave., New York, NY 10021. "High-end small antiques shop that has the most wonderful one-of-a-kind things you have ever seen."
▶**Denton and Gardner,** 60 Grand St., New York, NY 10013. "One of the most amazing collections of vintage European oil paintings. Some are Paris flea market finds."
▶**Judith Racht Gallery,** 13707 Prairie Rd., Harbert, MI 49128; 269/469-1080. "Converted an old church into her studio. Sells contemporary art and antique furniture. Has an amazing energy for seeking out contemporary artists that fit in this big open space."
▶**Marston House,** 101 Main St., Wiscasset, ME 04578; 207/882-6010 or www.marstonhouse.com. "I've been there one time, and I loaded up the truck. She [the owner] has a wonderful eye for old furniture and unique things. All of Wiscasset is a testament to the eye behind the business."
▶**Marston Luce,** 161 Wisconsin Ave. NW, Washington, D.C. 20007; 202/333-6800. "Very fine continental antiques shop with a lot of painted furnishings, tables, chairs, commodes, and lamps. It almost has a Swedish feel with painted floors and painted walls."

100 FROM FORD BOYD BAILEY:
"I can't say I have favorite stores, but I do love strolling through the shops in Charleston, South Carolina, and I love Magazine Street in New Orleans. Miami Circle in Atlanta is always an education. When I'm in a new city, I love exploring the galleries and antiques shops."

112 FROM MADELINE ROTH:
▶**Antique and Artisan Center,** 69 Jefferson St., Stamford, CT 06902; 203/327-4858. Madeline likes to shop for antiques in this area of Connecticut, but especially at this center. "You can't even get through it all in a day."
▶**Bergdorf Goodman,** 754 Fifth Ave., New York, NY; 212/753-7308. Madeline likes it because it's the only department store that isn't all over the U.S. "It's elegant and beautiful. It has really different things."
▶**Gallagher's Vintage Magazine Store,** 126 E. 12th St., New York, NY 10003; 212/473-0840 or

STYLE CLOSE TO HOME When you love style and live off the beaten path, finding design help and seeing great style may require a bit of ingenuity. Here's how:
▶ Visit local stores. You might find that local person with great style dressing a window at a clothing store, planting window boxes at the nursery, or selling their wares at an antiques mall. If you like the style, ask who did the work. Many of the designers featured in *Trade Secrets* expanded their design talents thanks to customers who noticed their work.
▶ Read the local paper. Watch for features on local homes and businesses. Take note of new design-related businesses in your area.
▶ Attend seasonal open houses and garden tours. You'll gather lots of ideas and maybe the name of a designer who might be able to help you with a project.
▶ Become a web sleuth. The world is at your fingertips thanks to websites that offer a peek at products and tell you how to get them home. For starters, search under furniture, home decorating, antiques, and fabric.

www.vintagemagazines.com. The store sells fashion magazines from the early 1900s to present. "This is where you stock up. Call them up if you're looking for vintage fashion magazines."
▶**Bill Kohanek Antiques,** 121 W. State St., Geneva, IL 60134; 630/232-0552. "He has wonderful things."
▶**Laduree** (pastry shop), 16 Rue Royale, Paris (8), France 33–1; 42 60 21 79. "The shop is just beautiful. Everything is in mint green or a purply pink."

124 FROM CINDI GAETKE:
▶**Dailey-Grommé Antiques,** 208 King St., Charleston, SC 29401; 843/853-2299. "I'm just like a kid in a candy store," says Cindi. The store stocks Art Deco pieces that she buys for herself and for clients. "It's just as much fun for me to see it in someone else's house as it is to own it."
▶**Lady Tess Everlasting Florals,** 2004 Wappoo Dr., Charleston, SC 29412; 843/762-3999. "She does a lot of dried flowers that look incredible."

132 FROM SCHNEIDER/EULAU:
▶**Barneys New York;** 888/822-7639 for store locations. "The standards are unbelievable." Look for clothing, jewelry, and gifts.
▶**Colette,** 213 Rue Saint Honoré, Paris, France; www.colette.fr/index.php. "They sell everyday objects and treat them like art." Fragrance, fashion, shoes, and objects.
▶**10 Corso Como,** Milan. This grand bazaar sells everything from Moroccan slippers to Indian rugs. They sell lots of objects, but mostly fashion.
▶**DeVera,** 29 Maiden Ln., San Francisco, CA 94108; 415/788-0828. Fredrico DeVera hand-picks

and displays everything from Italian glass to jewelry in his shop. "It's whatever he loves."
▶**Kitson,** 115 S. Robertson, Los Angeles, CA 90048; 310/859-2652. For information about stores on Robertson, see www.stylemaven.com. "It's pop culture. The store sells very happening objects—clothes, candles, and body stuff."

142 FROM D'ETTE COLE:
▶**Big Red Sun,** 1102 E. Cesar Chavez, Austin, TX 78702; 512/480-9749. "It's a cool garden place that takes a really different approach. I like to see how they use vintage planters or other items in the garden."
▶**Central Home Goods,** 512 Rio Grande, Austin, TX 78701; 512/476-1010. "New and old stuff and custom upholstery."
▶**Newark International Antiques Fair,** Newark, England; www.dmgantiquefairs.com. This show features 4,000 exhibitors. "It's a huge show. Since I've been doing this for eight years now, I have people who buy for me there and I make the rounds seeing them and what they have found for me."
▶**Provence area in France.** "There are a couple of big antiques fairs, but mainly I have to really beat the bushes. I go to small town markets all over and spend every day buying. It's a lot of hard work but I love French textiles, books, dishes, and paintings. It's a beautiful place to be working so hard."
▶**Room Service Vintage,** 107 E. North Loop Blvd., Austin, TX 78751; 512/451-1057. "Although its stock is more in the 1950s to 1970s era, I rarely leave there empty-handed."

▶**Round Top Warrenton Antiques Shows** (twice yearly). Marburger Farm Antique Show, Round Top, TX. Call 800/947-5799 or check www.roundtop-marburger.com. Round Top Antiques Fair, Round Top, TX. Call 281/493-5501 or check www.roundtopantiquesfair.com. "It's always such a treasure hunt there. I especially like Marburger Farms and try never to miss their Tuesday morning opening. It's such a conflict of interest for me since I'm either supposed to be setting up my show or selling my stuff instead of being out shopping!"

▶**Uncommon Objects,** 1512 S. Congress Ave., Austin, TX 78704; 512/442-4000. "I'm not just saying it's the best locally because it is my shop. I never know what great thing I'm going to score there. My business partner and I hand-picked this group of dealers, and it was often because they were people that we were buying from at other shops or shows."

150 FROM SCHLUPP/SEMKE:
SOURCES
All furniture, accessories, light fixtures, and artwork from Mig and Tig; 312/644-8277 or www.migandtig.com.

160 FROM VERSCHOOR/SAUNIER:
▶**Brimfield.** For J&J Promotions, Brimfield, MA. Call 413/245-3436 or check www.jandj-brimfield.com. For Brimfield May's Antique Market, Inc., call 413/245-9271 or check www.maysbrimfield.com. "Brimfield has tons and tons of stuff."
▶**First Monday Trade Days,** Canton, TX; 903/451-1057 or www.firstmondaycanton.com. This is the self-proclaimed world's oldest and largest flea market.
▶**Flea markets anywhere.** "I'll stop by any I see. It's not where you go, it's what you buy."
▶**Holland and Belgium** for general antiquing. "Pickers there know us and buy for us all year."
▶**Lille, France** (A 48-hour, continuous flea market in August). "Lille transforms itself into a giant flea market once a year."

170 FROM JIMMIE CRAMER:
▶**Beaver Creek Antiques Market,** 20202 National Pike, Hagerstown, MD 21740; 301/739-8075 or www.beavercreekantiques.com. "It's where I rent a booth."
▶**D.C. Big Flea,** Dulles Expo Center, Chantilly, VA.; www.damorepromotions.com. "Very reasonable prices. Great variety. It's more flea market than antiques show."
▶**E-bay;** www.ebay.com. "That's where I got a lot of garden stuff," he says.
▶**Edward & Edward,** 35 S. Carroll St., Frederick, MD 21701; 301/695-9674. "Consignment shop with great prices. It has a wide variety with some architectural pieces."
▶**Ekster Antiques,** 105 S. King St., Leesburg, VA 20176; 703/771-1784 or www.eksterantiques.com. "European pieces and great accessories."
▶**Greater York Antiques Show,** York, PA; 717/397-7209. "Good country stuff. You don't go buying to resell, you go to buy for yourself."
▶**Morgan Park** (old Oatlands Show), Dordy

Fontinel; Leesburg,. VA; 703/779-2800. "Everything from collectibles to top antiques. There's something for everyone."
▶**New Oxford Antique Center,** 333 Lincolnway W., New Oxford, PA 17350; 717/624-7787. "Really good country pieces."
▶**Old Glory Antique Marketplace,** 5862 Urbana Pike, Frederick, MD 21704; 301/662-9173. "I always find something there."
▶**Thanksgiving Farm Garden Center,** 1619 Buckeystown Pike, Adamstown, MD 21710; 301/662-1291. "They're always up-to-date with the new plants."

184 FROM JOETTA MOULDEN:
▶**Adkins Architectural Antiques,** 3515 Fannin, Houston, TX 77004; 713/522-6547. "Salvaged architectural fragments—doors, windows, tubs, sinks, faucet sets, and old hardware. You never know what you will find," Joetta says.
▶**Balinskas Architectural Imports,** 242 W. 19th St., Houston, TX 77008; 713/880-4774. "Ethnic and exotic antique wood carvings, window frames, beds, benches, mirrors, and accessories."
▶**Brian Stringer Antiques,** 2031 West Alabama, Houston, TX 77098; 713/526-7380. "Wonderful shop with antique baskets, chandeliers, artwork, and good English pine pieces."
▶**Design District,** 2620 Joanel, Houston, TX 77027; 713/840-9877. "Unusual accessories, large-scale rustic and earthy vessels, slipper chairs, terrific bath products, stationery, and mirrors."
▶**John Holt Antiques,** 2416 Woodhead, Houston, TX 77019. "Furniture and unusual 18th-and 19th-century antiques from Mexico and Spain."
▶**Kuhl-Linscomb,** 2424 West Alabama, Houston, TX 77098; 713/526-6000. "Antiques, decorative accessories, bath props, and tabletop. Unusual."
▶**Old Katy Road Antiques,** 9198-B Old Katy Rd., Houston, TX 77055, 713/461-8124. "Great small mall full of small pieces of furniture as well as art and accessories."
▶**Que Milagro,** 2913 Ferndale Place, Houston, TX 77098; 713/521-3591. "She has 18th- and 19th-century santos, retablos, and ex-votos from Mexico, which I collect," says Joetta.
▶**Reeves Antiques,** 2415 Taft, Houston, TX 77006; 713/523-5577. "Auction and estate-sale items at good prices."
▶**Surroundings,** 1710 Sunset Blvd., Houston, TX 77005; 713/527-9838. "Great ethnic accessories, hand-painted furniture and mirrors, exotic kilim rugs, nicho shelves, furniture and crafts from Morocco, South America, Mexico, and Indonesia."
▶**Tu Chez,** 1906 West Alabama, Houston, TX 77098; 713/533-0818. "Unexpected selection of home furnishings, terrific lamps. Antiques and new."
SOURCES
Hand-painted rug: Lisa Frisco, 5308 Piping Rock, Houston, TX 77056; 713/965-9047.

192 FROM MARY MULCAHY:
"I always go shopping on Clemente Street in San Francisco rather than the touristy Chinatown. I love to go to the flea markets in the San Francisco

Bay area when I can catch them. Nothing is better than a good Vermont auction, though. I've also found a few treasures with French heritage by scouring the small towns of Quebec province."
▶**Arch,** 99 Missouri St., San Francisco, CA 94107; 415/433-2724. "Great art store and really fun miscellaneous stuff."
▶**Boulangerie Bay Bread,** 2325 Pine St., San Francisco, CA 94115; 415/440-0356. "They're the best pastries in the world."
▶**Flea markets in Hudson,** Quebec (outside Montreal).
▶**Ichiban Kan,** 22 Peace Plaza, San Francisco, CA 94115. "It's like a dollar store in Japan town in San Francisco, and they always have new and delightful finds."
▶**Interieur Perdu,** 340 Bryant Street, San Francisco, CA 94107; 415/543-1616. "Great vintage things from Europe, mostly French."
▶**Studio Encanto,** 1055 N. Oracle Road, Tucson, AZ 85704; 520/318-9300. "Accessories, fragrance, and home furnishings."
▶**Sue Fisher King,** 3067 Sacramento St., San Francisco, CA 94115; 415/922-7276. "Great selection of accessories."
▶**Tom's Furniture Store,** 5454 E. Pima St., Tucson, AZ 85716; 520/795-5210. "Used furniture, estate sale items. Lots to look at."

204 FROM LYNN STEELY:
▶**Andy Newcom** (by appointment only), Kansas City, MO; 816/444-6047. Paintings and other artwork (paintings in dining room).
▶**The Curious Sofa,** 329 Southwest Blvd., Kansas City, MO 64108; 816/221-6600 "Garden statuary and coral."
▶**5th Street Antiques,** 122 W. 5th, Kansas City, MO 64106; 816/472-9700. Outstanding Victorian iron garden urns, wonderful Victorian textiles, and big furniture with carving. "Mike Peters, who owns the shop, is a larger-than-life character who is always outrageous."
▶**The Flea,** I-435 & Front Street, Kansas City, MO; 800/252-1501. "Monthly flea market and antiques show."
▶**John Scott Antiques** (by appointment only), Kansas City, MO; 816/591-0442. "Lots of stuff including Chinese furniture."
▶**Jack Zeman** (by appointment only), Los Angeles, CA; 323/666-3333. Photographer and antiques dealer.
▶**Local garage and estate sales.** "Oooh, so much from those."
▶**Marburger Farm Antique Shows;** Round Top, TX; 800/947-5799. "Leather chairs and iron garden urns."
▶**20th Century Furniture, Objects & Art** (by appointment only), P.O. Box 410875, Kansas City, MO 64141; 816/471-7677. Carries modern furniture, great vintage artwork, and good Navajo rugs. "Owner Nick Carter is always at the forefront of trends."
▶**Target.** "Small, clean-looking decorative accessories, especially for bath and kitchen."

214

index